Shooting From The Heart

Also by Rob Goldman

Beauty Unconscious

Shooting From The Heart

Creating Passion And Purpose
In Your Life And Work

ROB GOLDMAN

Center for Creative Development
Huntington, New York

For Carol

CONTENTS

Our deepest fear is not that we are inadequate.

Our deepest fear is that we are powerful beyond measure.

It is our light, not our darkness that most frightens us.

We ask ourselves, who am I to be brilliant,

gorgeous, talented, fabulous?

Actually, who are you not to be?

You are a child of God.

Your playing small does not serve the world.

There is nothing enlightened about shrinking

so that other people won't feel insecure around you.

We are all meant to shine, as children do.

We were born to make manifest the glory of God that is within us.

It is not just in some of us; it is in everyone.

And as we let our own light shine, we unconsciously

give other people permission to do the same.

As we are liberated from our own fear,

our presence automatically liberates others.

—Marianne Williamson
Return to Love, p. 165

ACKNOWLEDGMENTS

I would like to give special thanks to Jeff Logan, my teacher and friend. This book is the result of countless hours of recorded conversations that I shared with Jeff. His knowledge of all that is yoga—his wisdom, compassion, and incomparable listening—made those conversations some of the most enlightening of my life. Without Jeff, this book would not exist.

I would also like to thank my wife, Carol, the rock who grounds my perpetual roll. Carol, I love you dearly.

Franz Feige, my spiritual teacher and guide, thank you for leading me painstakingly toward presence and for helping me to trust.

Luke DeLalio, for so much support in so many ways. You are one of the most generous, talented people I've ever had the privilege to call my friend.

Ronen Yaari, for your dedication to creating a full and balanced life. You are a wonderful friend!

Ellen Fleury, for your never-ending design talents and even more so, your never-ending willingness to help.

Bea Vanni, for your tireless, brilliant editing of this five-year gift to myself.

Gabriel Halpern, for your ever-wise counsel, "If you want to be happy, create!"

Sheila Walsh and St. Joseph's Renewal Center, for your warm hospitality during several years of this book's writing.

Michael (Sprocket) Kaufman, for your selfless support, kindness and care.

Mitch Holsborg, for your undying belief in my success and dogged insistence that this book be written.

Richard Gardner, for helping me to realize the true potential of Shooting From The Heart.

Mom, they say that the only thing a mother really needs to do well is to truly love her children. They're right! Thank you, you've succeeded beyond your wildest dreams.

Dad, some things are definitely worth finishing! Not all, but this one for sure. Thank you for caring so much, listening so well, and believing in me through it all. I love you.

INTRODUCTION

How do you define creativity? Time and time again, I hear the same self-disparagement, "I can't paint. I can't sing. I can't act. I'm just not creative." Creativity is certainly not limited to those with particular artistic talent. No, creative genius lies within us *all*, and it begs to be awakened!

A so-called *work of art* represents an external expression of your truest self, organically born from within. The miraculous offspring of your own being embraces slivers of your soul, set free to adorn the world. Your creative ability is profound!

This book will help open your eyes to the limits you unconsciously place on your creative potential. It will challenge you to step outside the box you've labeled *me* and encourage and inspire you to explore the untapped magic and mystery of spirit—the whole of your being. You will learn how to replace old, unconscious habits with newfound, self-empowering actions. Instead of dreams about what could be or regrets of what might have been, embrace your God-given gifts and discover your life's purpose, commit to its actualization and swing into committed action.

As you embrace the beauty and freedom afforded by a dedicated practice, the shoulds, coulds and woulds of life are replaced by deep inner knowing and an astonishing sense of self. At last, you will come to know the real you and create from that place of love, integrity and wisdom.

Creative living implies an innovative approach to learning, problem solving, careers, relationships, parenting, prosperity, personal style, and so much more. It means recognizing opportunities that the universe offers and knowing when and how to seize them, without doubt or hesitation. Warning: They may not be what you were expecting.

So discover the miracle of your magnificence, with the wonder of a child and the wisdom of a sage. You owe it to yourself. You owe it to the world!

Namaste

Ferris Wheel, Huntington, New York

CHAPTER 1
COMING HOME

For many years, my photography assignments dispatched me to the most beautiful places in the western world. Clients the likes of Club Med, Cosmopolitan, Maxim, Brides Magazine, Nikon Camera, and Spa Finder summoned me to so-called paradise. Crews were coordinated—gorgeous models, hair and make-up artists, wardrobe and prop stylists, assistants—along with hundreds of pounds of clothing, props, and the finest photography equipment money could buy. Off we went to the land of make believe with a cast of fabulous faces and bodacious bodies in tow.

My job, my talent, in essence, fictionalized perfection. I received handsome payment for my photographs in magazines to convince millions that the lives they witness are absolutely real and readily attainable. You too can and *should* (unless, of course, you're a loser) awaken daily to Technicolor sunrises, perpetual laughter, and hand-in-hand strolls on endless beaches. My images convinced even the most Doubting Thomases that this was so.

In my heart I had become a photographic con artist, but what do you do when your work is well recognized and highly compensated? On the surface it seems like all's well, but beneath echoes certain emptiness and an undeniable calling toward another end, toward substance.

Change on the Horizon

On New Year's Eve 1994, my life took a radical turn. My first child, Gabriel Matthew Morris, came into the world, and I soon lost the zeal for all that is commercial photography. As I came to experience the inexpressible, genuine beauty of a new human life, I realized that I had conned myself along the way. I'd set myself up in a career that supported my own impossible quest for perfection. If I couldn't have the life that television and movies convinced me was absolutely attainable and normal, then I would create it photographically.

© *Marriott International Inc. Photo by Rob Goldman*

I felt swindled, and worse, I had perpetuated the sham. Jay Martin, in his landmark book, *Who am I This Time?*, explains, "Identification with fictions can become obsessive, monolithic, more or less permanent, unconditioned and unqualified…Fictions thus can provide a grandiose model for the self which otherwise experiences itself as impotent." Mass media has radically propagated and capitalized on our need to ease the aching sense of deficiency that has plagued our culture for the past 50 to 60 years.

There's No Place Like Home

It was just before sunrise, on a magnificent Martinique beach, that an arrow of enlightenment pierced my heart. As I stood, camera in hand, awaiting dawn's mystical glow, I experienced a sudden, incontrovertible realization. Boom! I was done. It was time to go home, literally and spiritually. Regardless of consequence, a greater force was at work and I simply could not deny destiny. My career as a commercial photographer was over and the painful process of metamorphosis had uninvitedly begun.

Carol, Gabriel and Eli

Learning to see *behind the curtain* requires diligent, often challenging work, beyond the enchantment of the quick fix. Persuasive messages fill our world with false promises and convince us that the antidote to our discontent and cure for our aching hearts remain just a phone call away.

Remember Dorothy's revelation when she's asked to reflect upon her lessons in Oz? Only after her difficult pursuit does revelation come her way: "If I ever go looking for my heart's desire again, I won't look any further than my own backyard, because if it isn't there, I never really lost it to begin with." She didn't dial 1-800-PRESCRIBED-BLISS and await the FedEx driver with miracle remedy in hand. No, Dorothy engaged in an earnest quest, confronted her fears, fought her demons and inevitably realized her truth.

Dorothy's sympathetic comrades, like overprotective mothers and well-meaning friends, wished her journey could have been less taxing. The Tin Man demanded that Glinda, the good witch, explain why she hadn't told Dorothy that she'd always had the means to return home. Dorothy, she explained, had to learn it for herself, by means of the only true teacher: full immersion in the wonderful, often-thorny experience of what my friend, Fig, aptly calls *living alive*. There are simply no shortcuts to revelation.

You can't learn to swim in a field was the wisdom once delivered to me in the form of a Chinese fortune cookie. Smart cookie, eh? Finding true meaning requires an experience of life beyond one's comfort zone.

Nike's tough advice to "Just Do It" urges us to confront fears and uncertainties and follow the often unpredictable yellow brick road.

When logic and strategy alone dictate action, results are strictly limited to what the intellect can realize. This approach is severely limited by what we already know and is often prejudiced with fear and egotism. Creativity, on the other hand, is fueled by the mystery of magnificence and trust in the unknowable. For many, the realization of our ultimate selves is painfully constrained by a lack of imagination and disconnection from spirit.

Finding Your Center

Education activist, Parker Palmer, speaks a great deal about the transition from what he terms "fear-based to faith-based knowledge", from the known to the mystical (*The Courage to Teach* 1998). Nowadays, with success solely measured by achievement, prudence feels all but innate. Assess the situation, calculate risk, and act only when the odds for success are notably in your favor. Failure is just not an option. The heartbreaking reality of such failsafe conditioning delivers a severe limitation of life experience.

The faith necessary to hazard oneself in the world, to boldly explore one's potential, is simply not supported by modern American convention—not in education, not in business, not in relationships.

Step-by-step programs and kits filled with flawless instructions to complete the perfect assembly line widget, uncover a culture of imagination relentlessly restricted. The prompts and possibilities for creativity eradicated, the invitation to imagination revoked: victory becomes the sole gauge of success. This model virtually guarantees a crippling of the creative process, fostering insecurity and doubt in place of the empowering faith of which Palmer speaks.

When the harsh meter of judgment turns off and the infinite nature of potentiality tunes in, the doors of awareness swing open and we return home to what the Buddha named, *The Island of Self*. In that fierce vastness, we may awaken to the sheer miracle of revelation.

Nothing compares to the infinite wonder at the core of your being. That is what makes your personal style your own. You are one-of-a-kind and responsible to discover, embrace and express your uniqueness, for your own benefit and that of the universe.

Unfortunately, your uniqueness has likely been buried under mounds of convolution, anxiety and confusion since your birth—obscured by rules of conformity and limitation, peer pressure, fears, insecurities, and in my case, destructively dualistic thinking that distorted my perception with an all or nothing precept.

Underneath all of your ideas and ideals hide the sanctity and magnificence of your authentic self. You cannot willfully decide the content or expression of its genuineness; they simply exist!

Coming home is returning to the here and now, being your complete self, where questions of right or wrong and good or bad never need enter the equation. Issues of approval do not exist. Fearful uncertainties cease. Gone are what ifs: What if I make a mistake? What if I look like a fool? What if they don't understand me? From this place called *home*, there is peaceful knowing and the incomparable strength and beauty of faithful confidence.

Letting Go

At a Keith Jarrett concert in Philadelphia, I sat next to Eddie Jones, an old-time jazz drummer. Jarrett, a jazz pianist, inarguably ranks as one of the most innovative improvisational artists alive. As he dove deeper and deeper into his playing, Jones dove deeper into his air drumming. The energy they both exuded enchanted me.

Jones described Jarrett as a *conduit*—a channel where the energy of the universe flows. What really struck us was how Jarrett lived beyond the music, even beyond himself. We realized that Keith Jarrett's talent relies on a principle that Jones explained as "You gots to get out the way!" You've got to learn to let go, to surrender and be guided by a greater voice.

Our Self-Imposed Prison

Jones's words struck a place of deep truth. The restrictions that we impose on ourselves through preconceived notions of logic-based outcomes often render us oblivious to life's greatest miracles, the unforeseen gifts of the universe. Tiptoeing through life in self-defeat— not ready, not now, not enough, not sure, not comfortable, not me— will likely lead to fear-driven compromises, resentment, anxiety, and regret. Instead, you can choose to embrace and explore your infinite potential. Create rather than react.

When I speak of letting go, I am often accused of being unrealistic. I hear all about the realities of people's lives and the impossibility of the pursuit of dreams. The truth is they are scared to death. They fear relinquishing control, fear change, fear the unknown, fear failure; fear letting go! Self-doubt and stubborn insistence fuel a self-defeating, self-fulfilling prophecy. The punishment: Life on a hamster wheel.

Many a child's upbringing is awkwardly shaped by the destructive four-letter word *can't*: You can't do that or you'll get hurt, can't wander away or you'll get lost, can't make a mistake or you'll let down your teammates. Can't, can't, can't! Conversely, the truth speaks you can; you should; you must.

From the moment of birth, well-meaning parents and caretakers lovingly protected you from harm of every sort. Yet, as we mature we feel compelled to free ourselves of the *can't* trap. When you consciously travel your own path, you realize that many of these rules have worn out their welcome. New, constructive guidelines must be self-initiated if you want to evolve into a fully actualized human being. This entails letting go, changing and growing.

Jeff, Huntington Harbor

Insightful teachers, rare as they are, will recognize the limitations that you place on yourself, the fear and habitual clinging that prevent your fullest expression. Ideally, you will then be encouraged to release fully into that expression—physically, emotionally and creatively, not as an act of reckless abandon, but as unreserved, intuitive movement within a specific set of parameters. The boundaries of some form or container become necessary in any spiritual endeavor and inevitably provide the means to ultimate freedom.

The depth and breadth of my philosophy are entwined in my Shooting From The Heart* program. Photography and yoga form the foundation of this body/mind/spirit process that is as flexible as it is prescribed. Photography uses the form of the frame; yoga uses the postures or *asanas*, as they're known in Sanskrit. We don't practice all 8,400,000 asanas, but rather a small selection to constantly test the limits of our restricted physical and mental perceptions, revealing hidden facets of our astonishing selves.

Envision a raging, wild river (anxiety, struggle, uncertainty) that flows through and is converted by some behavioral gateway (yoga, for example). This gateway is an alignment mechanism, a laboratory for contemplation and clarity. As water passes through that gateway, it transforms into a tranquil, blissful pond (peace, truth, knowing). The water is still water, just as you are still you, but your essence and energy have metamorphosed. You have evolved.

I spent seven years photographing nude women on a black background, in one room, with one window, with one lens, and one film. Within that limited, refined form, through that *gateway*, I discovered untold possibilities and an entirely new level of bold, intimate expression. In that sanctified space, the artist in me was born.

Kim, New York City

CHAPTER 2
FEAR OF COMMITMENT

In an interview, a journalist asked me to recount the history of my teaching career. I recited the stages of my evolution one commitment at a time. My love and fascination for people really provoked my decision to major in photography at college, where my serious pursuit began toward a career in photography, specifically *people* photography.

I opened my own business as a commercial photographer due to my infatuation with people. I worked with diverse people: models, art directors, photo editors, crew. I spent hours delighting in the idiosyncrasies of humankind through observation, analysis, and photography. Eventually, my photography became very personal and totally connected with the essence and spirit of my subjects. Quite naturally, I ventured into the world of fine art photography where I offered a setting for people to simultaneously express their beauty, their power and their vulnerability.

Eventually, my passion for and union with others influenced my present commitment, inspiring people to unlock *their* creative potential. In retrospect, I see that my pursuits have echoed my own evolution. As I've grown, my needs have changed. To satisfy those needs, I have cultivated internal and external conditions for further growth. I've built better boxes.

Why We Battle Commitment

When given the freedom to choose, the only commitments to honor are those that stem from an inner knowing. Commitments made through false criteria satisfy one's ego alone and are destined to bring unhappiness, such as a career choice based solely on money or a spouse chosen for societal status. Decisions such as these will inevitably bring misery and suffering to anyone involved. They are insincere, founded on delusion, deception, and lies.

In *Awaken the Giant Within*, author Anthony Robbins writes of the power of decisions:

> More than anything else, I believe it's our *decisions*, not the *conditions* of our lives, that determine our destiny...My whole life changed in just one day—the day I determined not just what I'd *like* to have in my life or what I wanted to become, but when I *decided* who and what I was *committed* to having and being in my life.

Arriving at such commitments requires making the right choices. Choices based in Truth. It calls for courage, faith, and experience; for sacrifice, knowing, and compassion; for heightened intuition and passion. In addition, it requires an initial commitment to your own evolution and quest for deep satisfaction.

As you grow, your evolution will insist on changes of commitments. Don't fight the flow. A commitment at one point in your evolution may not be valid at another point, and it's a lie to not acknowledge your own development. Commitments are not always permanent. To declare you won't change simply because of a commitment you made does not honor your evolution. Evolution is our natural state.

Running away from a commitment that presents challenges denotes the antithesis of evolution, evasion. Challenges often present themselves for growth's sake. There is, after all, no such thing as a problem without a gift for you in its hands. The key is learning to differentiate the hurdles that are meant to be walked around from those that require transformation and those that demand obliteration.

I dedicated a career solely to fine art photography. I vowed to what I deeply felt to be right. As it turned out, that vow enabled me to delve so deeply into the inner workings of the creative process that today, I find myself committed to a very different vision. Today, I am a teacher, speaker, mentor, and coach, helping people unlock their creativity in areas of art, education, and business.

Seek a Higher Purpose

Today, I am following my true path, consistently tweaking my vision and taking action to bring my dreams to fruition. Teaching and creativity coaching offer me the most rewarding career I could imagine. Today, I feel truly successful. Photography still plays an important part of my life, but now I follow a different path. To ignore or doubt my path would be deceptive, painful, stressful and in fact, a lie.

In *The Path of Least Resistance*, author Robert Fritz explains:

> Perhaps there are people who in their imagination can hear even greater music than Beethoven's. But creators not only can imagine or envision, *they also have the ability to bring what they imagine into reality.* Once a creation exists, an evolutionary process can take place. Each past creation builds a foundation for the next creation.

Evolution occurs in stages. The struggles confronted as we climb from one plateau to the next are what Julia Cameron, author of *The Artist's Way*, terms "ugly-duckling growth stages." During these periods, we often feel lost and tend to dabble and procrastinate. Commit to discover, rediscover, and honor your authentic self and you will undoubtedly find those ugly ducklings lead to more and more gratifying situations along your true path. To your next commitments.

Your greatest effort should be to see into and through the barriers that prevent you from embracing a deep, inner knowing of your true self. As you feel the undeniable calling to move on, to evolve, fears will likely arise that aspects of your life are ending. Indeed, you experience a death of sorts. By quieting the mind and turning inward, untold mystical gifts mired in the muck and confusion reveal themselves. So do solace and divine guidance.

Our passions naturally lead us to certain commitments. Active engagement with them will likely lead to a surge of new knowledge, interests, and eventually, newfound passions. In turn, they may spawn other obligations, leaving the previous ones behind.

The wheels of transformation are set in motion with that process of dedication, letting go, rededication, creation, destruction and so on. Be forewarned: Ideals, possessions, and even people may get stranded in the wake of such motion. Nevertheless, this is our true nature. If you want to grow, be open to change. You evolve to what you understand from your heart to be truth, knowing that this truth too could change.

Jaime

Find Your Truth and Commit

It sounds like an oxymoron: the truth changes. Your understanding of Truth, meaning your personal truth, *does* change. It evolves. J. Krishnamurti, one of the greatest spiritual teachers of all time, said, "The most intelligent thing anyone can say is, I don't know." You really don't know where your evolution will lead you, but you can certainly sense when you have arrived at the next level. When that understanding is felt in the deepest recesses of your integrity, you know it is worthy of your commitment.

To make these commitments means living totally. No compromise. No delusion. You pledge to immerse yourself with total conviction to do the work necessary to make it a reality. There's nothing to say that five years later, you don't sit perplexed, thinking you thought you knew, but now you see differently. Congratulations, you've grown. You have evolved!

Through disciplined action, your commitments become unconditional and you may rejoice in the pleasure and fulfillment of your efforts. The work leaves no room for fear, doubt, or concession. You remain in pursuit of your greatest passions. While it is true that the road to realization requires significant struggle, sacrifice, discipline, and perseverance, the rewards are incomparable.

If left abstract, the pursuit of your dreams quickly becomes daunting and unimaginable. With a system in place, it is both possible and fun. Initially, commit to replace a chunk of time currently spent in mainte-

nance of your present condition and shift that eft
you really desire. As Robert Fritz writes:

> There is a profound difference between problem so.
> creating. Problem solving is taking action to have soi
> go away—the problem. Creating is taking action to have
> something come into creation—the creation.

A two-hundred foot oak began its life as a seed. The seed became a
seedling and ceased its life as a seed. Seed to seedling, to sapling, to saw
timber, to mighty oak. Your evolution begins with the first, most often
intimidating step, the impulse that jolts the boulder free and sends it
rolling down the mountain. Barbara Sher, author of *I Could Do Anything
If I Only Knew What It Was*, offers this judicious advice: "Start small,
start now."

To squelch the quest toward your dreams is to live tragically. Not only do
you rob yourself of your happiness when dreams go unfulfilled, you
deprive the universe of your greatest gifts and potential. The longer you
procrastinate, the greater the level of fear and rationalization to overcome,
and the longer you perpetuate the compromise of your happiness.

Oftentimes, our preconceived goals are not met. Our commitments
don't always lead us to the end that we envisioned. Through effort, a
willingness to try, failing, and trying again, we learn that experience
teaches us life's greatest lessons. Whether you win or lose, you will
certainly learn and grow.

...nit to living your life as it naturally evolves. Resolve to what you :now to be right and true with your heart as your guide. Only through that commitment can you hope to obtain a deep understanding of yourself, others and the world. As it is written in The Talmud, "You don't see things as they are; you see things as you are." Only by becoming intensely involved in the core of your work will you discover the intensity of your infinite, all-knowing, powerful self. From that place, anything is possible—one commitment at a time.

Lisa, Tuscany

CHAPTER 3
DISCIPLINE IS FREEDOM

From an early age, I studied classical piano. Each week, I took lessons, and my parents expounded on the importance of regular practice. After twelve years of training, I became a proficient, classical pianist. In retrospect, I thank my parents for their harassment. Undoubtedly, I would have abandoned my training otherwise, and I would not enjoy the pleasure that playing offers me today. Unfortunately, I did not possess that same discipline in my later pursuit of jazz improvisation.

Without the irksome support of my parents and left to my own devices, my young adult studies lasted only months. I was deluded by my desire for instant success. I lacked the patience and motivation necessary to excel. I live to regret it, as I am still frequently frustrated and long to play jazz. No hoping and wishing will make it so. There is only one way: Do the work.

Instant Gratification Brings Hardship

In *Light on Yoga*, yoga master B.K.S. Iyengar explains:

> Both the good and the pleasant present themselves to men and prompt them to action. The yogi prefers the good to the pleasant. Others driven by their desires prefer the pleasant to the good and miss the very purpose of life.

Since the dawn of mass media, the need for immediate satisfaction has been thrust upon us. False promises of instantaneous and effortless results make it too easy to become a victim of convenience and laziness. Advertisements demoralize the value of dedicated effort, promising everything from perfect bodies to perfect moods to perfect lives. They offer instantaneous, miraculous results—all without doing any work.

Whip out a credit card and this flawless world can be yours for just four easy payments. Even if you can't afford this miracle product, don't bother to earn money to pay for it. No, put yourself into debt. Certainly another miracle product will appear next week to effortlessly pay off your credit card.

My son understands a credit card as something to use when we've run out of money. To him, it's the ultimate instant gratification tool. He has no concept that with interest we'll actually pay considerably more in the long run, financially and emotionally. Corporate America has taken full advantage to preserve comfort as a primary human motivator.

With so many people living outside of what is right for them; the concepts of work and discipline often assume negative connotations. Discipline actually has its roots in the Latin, *disciplina*, meaning instruction or knowledge. Later, it changed to mean the maintenance of order necessary for giving instruction. When viewed in these terms, discipline assumes a totally positive connotation—an organized system for learning. Nothing to shy away from there.

Human nature seems to warrant that we derive our essential needs in an effortless way. Children learn the art of manipulation as their first means of coping. When an infant is hungry, she cries. Upon crying, she is fed. Very quickly, she learns how to direct this control to get more of what she needs to alleviate her discomfort. Eventually, she realizes quite instinctively that she can get just about anything by crying. Granted, it may be the only method available to her, but nonetheless, manipulation at its most primal.

Well-guided children learn that such behavior past toddlerhood is inappropriately selfish. A child's healthy development requires responsible role models of honorable behavior. Ideally, loving parents first fill that role, followed by wise teachers, mentors, and elders. Today's role models, however, often miss the mark: stressed out parents with conflicting priorities; sports figures as greedy, narcissistic tycoons; teachers with tenure who lazily ride out the duration of their careers.

Freedom Offers Choice

Living in a democracy, we are endowed with the freedom of choice. Freedom to walk a disciplined path offers but one choice, the path of truth. Discipline brings a quiet, peaceful mind and a sense of freedom, where you are free to act creatively, rather than reactively. Without discipline, your ideas and thoughts do not manifest. They are squandered.

Indeed, discipline is freedom, but what are you free from? Freedom from anything implies restriction, not freedom; your freedom is based on reactions to existing circumstances. Freedom in the most sincere terms means consciously and passionately reveling in your truth with complete knowledge that your actions are the best possible for your own good and the good of the universe.

Unfortunately, your truth has likely become distorted over time—by parents, teachers, friends, and mass media. Until one day you bewilderingly ask, "Who am I?" a question that for most people is a daunting and dangerous one likely to upset the status quo.

Difficult and painful, the process of excavating your truth requires extraordinary support and patience from those closest to you. Genuine happiness becomes impossible to find without coming to terms with that truth. Living a lie leaves you stranded in an unbalanced world of unbearable negativity and dis-integration.

In an essay regarding the work of Thomas Merton, Richard Fournier writes, "Our culture encourages us to identify with this false self, to walk around like 'skin encapsulated egos' (to borrow Alan Watts' picturesque phrase), feeling separate from one another, and attempting to fill our emptiness through the consumption of objects."

So yes, freedom is scary. It's much easier and more comfortable to be told what to do. To embrace discipline as positive motivation, you must be able to welcome what freedom entails: A world without bottled questions and answers, and thereby, a world of infinite potential.

Create Systems for Your Success

With so many possibilities, a certain structure becomes necessary to maintain momentum and be carried toward success. Set parameters for an accessible, manageable framework. For example, this book exists as the result of a precisely defined method:

1. Organization of my insights, one concept at a time.

2. Individual concepts assessed one chapter at a time.

3. First draft scrutinized and edited to refine my meaning.

4. Quotes, photographs, and testimonials gathered with its bibliography.

5. The design of the book's other aspects completed.

6. Self-imposed, publicized deadlines insured timely completion.

This device works for me, advancing my efforts from an abstract jumble to a finished product. Discipline and structure become married partners.

In the making of Apocalypse Now, director Francis Ford Coppola pled with a young, unruly Dennis Hopper the necessity of a disciplined approach. Hopper refused to learn his lines, insisting on the merits of his improvisational skills. A wiser Coppola explained, "If you know your lines, then you can forget them…It's not fair to forget them if you never knew them."

The impetus for discipline must stem from your truth or remain an endless struggle. When I asked Jeff Logan, my yoga teacher, how he gets himself to practice yoga every day, he explained, "I don't even think of it that way. I look forward to it. It's what I do. It's who I am." Jeff's discipline, both self-imposed and nurturing, requires a significant degree of compassion for others and himself. The discipline becomes a welcomed practice.

A disciplined existence offers us the freedom to create rather than react to external pressures of blame or accountability. Reactions of any kind prove counterproductive and lead toward contempt, anxiety, and grief. I explained to my neighbor, Diane, the consequences of not putting her own mental, physical, and spiritual health at the forefront of her responsibilities. I cited the airliner announcement about how the oxygen masks drop from overhead in case of a loss of cabin pressure. When I asked her to recall the flight attendant's announcement, Diane replied, "Yeah, I know, put on your child's mask and then put on your own." Confused, she neglects her own essential needs.

Listen that Right Actions Follow

Right action results from the act of listening—listening with all of your senses. When you are present and totally connected, soulfully listening with compassion and respect, your actions come without thought. As they are sincerely right actions, they cannot be judged as good or bad, right or wrong.

Our conscious, prudent choices play a significant role in our own potentially joyous destinies. First, we must master control of our actions and reactions. As Benjamin Disraeli said, "Man is not the creature of circumstances; circumstances are the creature of men." Our acceptance and love of ourselves provides the freedom and clarity to act justly and constructively toward others.

Many unruly children, for instance, may require greater support and compassion than their average counterparts, rather than restrictions to keep them under control. Creative outlets for their intense behavior would provide structure instead of stilting their imaginations. Recent statistics show that nearly 3 million children in the U.S. use Ritalin to cope with Attention Deficit Hyperactivity Disorder (ADHD). The Journal of the American Medical Association recently revealed Ritalin as having addictive qualities and cardiac side effects similar to those of cocaine.

Nonetheless, production of Ritalin has increased more than sevenfold in the past eight years, and 90 percent is consumed in the United States, reports Time Magazine. All too often, healthy children who think and act *outside the box*, expressing themselves in a creative, perhaps somewhat manic way, are *tamed* to function within the system, while pharmaceutical companies make billions. Institutionalized schooling has few ways of dealing with such children. Rather, there is a calamity of mass sedation fostering compliance, not creativity. These devastating reactions suffocate the creativity of millions of children, sometimes the most gifted of all.

Importance of Discipline

The purpose of discipline is to enable us to thrive within our truth. It moves us toward leading responsible lives of the utmost integrity. Responsible to whom? To ourselves! So we become whole, strong, and ultimately capable of giving. Certainly discipline serves us individually, but its energy also rebounds back to the world.

A mother, for example, whose guilt obliges her to act the role of the perfect caregiver, lives not in truth but invariably in disgust and resentment to everyone's detriment. On the other hand, a mother who genuinely thrives on her children's pleasure will, out of earnest love, find immeasurable bliss and gratification in her own life. She's living her truth. Her devotion reflects an act of unconditional love.

Right-Sizing Discipline for You

There is only one right level of discipline for you at any given point in your development. At a yoga retreat I attended with master teacher Kofi Busia, a student asked if Kofi would share his diet regime with the class because she admired his apparently balanced life. Kofi explained that his diet, appropriate only for him, had evolved as he had evolved.

He explained that a Fortune 500 corporate executive would order surf and turf and a $400 bottle of wine at a business dinner because his choices are aligned with his lifestyle, as Kofi's are with his. For Kofi, vegetarianism and abstention from alcohol are aligned with his values and perspective. He encouraged the woman to honor her evolution and strive toward greater awareness, so she could consciously choose the diet proper for her.

A disciplined life allows for choices. It turns dreams into reality by offering a purposeful structure for action. It provides a responsible means and defines paths that enable you to create rather than manage a life, which weaves reactions through a maze of circumstances. You come to welcome your own chosen guidelines that propel you toward a happier, more fulfilling existence.

Many artists view the words structure, discipline, and responsibility as painful restrictions—enemies of the creative process. In comparison, the successful, prolific artist learns that without such boundaries, the pursuit of any creation becomes overwhelming and the artist is left to perpetually dabble and stray.

As diva Beverly Sills reminds us, "There are no short cuts to any place worth going." Vast difference persists between limiting the creative process itself and limiting innumerable choices which lead to freedom within the creative process. Your discipline gives you the confidence to constantly avert the lure of delusion or sway of apprehension, countless cravings or temptations. Joe Jackson's lyrics face the dilemma head-on in his song, "It's All Too Much":

I'd like to get to know
All the people I could be
If I just had the time
I could find out which one is me
Maybe I need religion
Or meditation 'til I disappear
They say that choice is freedom
I'm so free I'm stuck in therapy
And you know why—it's all too much

Following the path of your truest self requires considerable discipline, but only there can your heart lead you in the right direction. Once you embrace discipline for its own sake, sacrifice becomes a sincere process, not an imposition or restriction. Fatty, greasy foods, for example, don't fit into your life once you have consciously adopted a healthy diet. Mindless obedience loses its appeal as you stand on your own two feet and fall in love with the beauty of your individuality.

Paranoia demands excessive safety or conformity; it batters and imprisons the soul. When abused by incompetent leaders—egocentric managers, resentful parents, and deluded teachers—discipline is terribly destructive. Such hurtful misconstructions are often rooted in fear that the subject will rebel against norms that the ruler deems incontestable.

Truth exists for neither the ruler nor the ruled in this flawed rendition of discipline. It absolutely rejects the possibilities for creativity. It leaves room neither for elation or desolation—two requisites for a passionate existence. If it is our responsibility as human beings to be free and ultimately content, then this type of constricting behavior can be neither natural or respectable.

If parents, as a result of their own insecurities and fears, prolong oppressive levels of restraint, their children enter a torturous, self-perpetuating cycle. They will unavoidably develop into narrow-minded, apprehensive adults.

Alfred Stieglitz, often referred to as 'the father of modern photography,' said, "The greatest geniuses are those who have kept their childlike spirit and added to it breadth of vision and experience." Healthy discipline propels you toward that idyllic blend of wisdom and spontaneity.

With a disciplined practice, your creative potential is unlimited. So be still and listen to the essence of your soul. Fearlessly embracing your truth will liberate your extraordinary power. Creating, by its very definition, offers no known path, but *through the work*, the path presents itself. As the Taoist saying goes, "For health and happiness, everything in life is to be enjoyed. To keep enjoying it, take everything in moderation, including moderation!" Discipline as well.

El Encanto, Costa Rica

CHAPTER 4
MASTERY

At a certain point in my life, it was time for me to meet personally with several heroes whose successes I had admired only from afar. This modeling, as I understood, was to identify with my mentors' core beliefs.

First on my list was a brilliant photographer, Rodney Smith, who had achieved and maintained admirable notoriety over a lengthy and diverse photography career. Mr. Smith met my request with open arms to join him at his home. I visited only twice, each for a brief time, but I learned more about mastery in those few hours than in any other experience in my life. Smith was the real deal! Authenticity, dedication, and perseverance oozed from his body, his work, his home, his way. He walked the walk.

Allegiance to his personal style in every aspect of his life and work overwhelmed me. His relaxed confidence pervaded his presence like none I'd ever experienced. In the presence of greatness—a *master*—I felt comforted and inspired. My intuition guided me to the right teacher whose words were few, yet critical and keenly perceptive.

Practice, Practice, Practice

Smith focused solely on helping me. I reaped uncanny rewards simply by being in his presence. This man's relentless commitment to uncompromising authenticity and excellence moved me. His repeated mantra, "It's all about the work," became my guiding light from that point on. It's a constant reminder of the value of a committed effort to my deepest calling, regardless of the challenge. It reminds me of an old joke about a symphony conductor's reply to a disoriented pedestrian asking, "How do I get to Carnegie Hall?" "Practice, practice, practice," the conductor replied unpretentiously.

Practice in the west is most often seen as a process leading to an eventual outcome—the means to an end, an exam to be aced or an athletic competition to be won. When appreciated at a deeper level, it becomes evident that practice it is for its own sake. Such practice is the work of which Rodney Smith speaks. The work has its own rewards and satisfaction with no attachment to a predetermined outcome. Once a commitment is made, only focused practice enables progress toward mastery, and mastery is a ceaseless process.

Our initial efforts to learn require a great deal of concentration, willful exertion, and the elimination of burdensome temptations, but this conscientious restraint inevitably encumbers a natural flow of intuitive, creative energy. Mastery can only advance when intentional effort ceases and doing reaches becoming. The concentrative aspect of the work eventually transcends into complete absorption where the practitioner may indeed *become* the practice, the musician is one with his instrument, the dancer one with the dance.

Signs of Mastery

The title of "Master" speaks to those few who have earned it through intense, singular dedication. They discovered and embraced their calling, an extension of their truest selves, and consciously devoted themselves to their life's work. Through significant experience they came to know every aspect of their craft in depth, allowing them inside of their work.

My friend, Wesley Carter, an amazing woodworker, speaks about wood with a burning passion generally reserved for lovers. It's safe to say that Wesley is in love with, and is one with, wood. His passion and motivation for knowledge and experience in fine woodworking remains boundless.

Unfortunately, in our high-tech age, the reign of the master is disappearing. The value and recognition of mastery withers as industrialization grows and computerization takes over. Speed and price commonly outweigh the values of fine craftsmanship.

A 93-year-old Japanese carpenter explained to me that his lumber methodically ages at the bottom of a lake for 80 years. Not exactly what I'd call instant gratification! His respect for the natural world and uncompromised quality enthralled me as his perpetual grin gave testimony to his path toward a fulfilling life. What compels the master to relentless practice to the point of obsession in his quest toward mastery?

Transformation Emerges

Ultimately, the perfected yoga pose, the well-crafted wing chair, and the fine photograph get left behind. The form drops out as the pursuit of mastery leads to self-realization. What began as a willful undertaking becomes an act of transformation. The individual identity is dissolved, giving rise to an expanded state of consciousness where the unity of our being is the reward of our efforts. Consistent effort toward perfection matters most, not perfection itself.

Mastery is a humbling endeavor and requires a certain degree of faith as you surrender to an incomprehensible power. Practice setting your ego and expectations aside and embracing life as it evolves on its own accord. Remember, "You gots to get out the way," like the carpenter who's learned to listen to the lumber, the stone that guides the sculptor's chisel, or the mystical voice that brings forth your next brilliant idea.

Mastery can best be realized as an ever deepening, lifelong pursuit rather than an attainment. Refreshing beauty grows out of such a goalless process, as you progress forward toward higher levels of your greatest self.

Janessa, New York City

Self-Confidence Encourages Excellence

Dedication to an explicit pursuit enables us to excel and allows our sense of self-confidence to build on a solidly earned foundation. As *The Swordsman and the Cat*, an old book on swordplay, explains, "Teaching is not difficult, listening is not difficult either, but what is truly difficult is to become conscious of what you have in yourself and be able to use it as your own."

"Go confidently in the direction of your dreams," wrote Emerson. "Live the life you've imagined." You offer the most of yourself when you come from a place of heightened self-confidence. Confidence means committing to do versus wanting to do. The difference between saying, "I'll give it a try" and declaring, "I will do it" is the difference that makes great things happen. It is a radically different energy. Only through dedicated, focused effort can you honor your declaration to do with a deep appreciation of your capability and your entitlement to what you deem success.

We must learn the incomparable benefits of study under masterful teachers. Teachers in ancient cultures were not questioned; they earned the right of Master through decades of dedicated experience and commitment. Their wisdom had great depth.

Experience as a Motivator to Change

In our modern society, such honor and value of an apprentice-master relationship has all but disappeared. Our education system rather rewards rote knowledge conveyed in a vacuum. Countless students pay astronomical sums to advance their learning in sterile halls of knowledge, striving for that proverbial 4.0 in pursuit of a vital piece of paper. But in the end, did they come close to optimizing four, five or six years of life experience for that exorbitant price tag?

Our entire education system simply does not emphasize or appreciate mastery for teachers or students. Instead, over-intellectualization and the quest for high-paying jobs steer the process. Development of a deep connection with life is not included in the syllabus. From grade school on, the average child's education is spattered with occasional field trips to museums and zoos. What about spending time in the real world, navigating the physical, social, emotional, and intellectual challenges of life itself?

Missing in the education equation is hands-on, get down in the mud, life experience for students as well as for teachers. A history teacher, for example, could experience the world she teaches about by visiting or living in the places where such history was made. When a teacher's wisdom is acquired through firsthand experience, they can inspire a more informed, passionate learning environment. If only our education system would value and support such a philosophy, teachers would be required to live what they teach. Again, to walk the talk.

There's a wonderful Tao poem that speaks of such experience:

> An old man sits on a granite step.
> He plucks a treasured guitar.
> The strings throb with feeling;
> He needs no audience to open his heart.
> A boy enthusiastically wants to learn his style.
> "Style?" asks the man slowly. "My style is made of
> The long road of life, of heartbreak
> And joy, and people loved, and loneliness.
> Of war and its atrocities.
> Of a baby born.
> Of burying parents and friends.
> My scale is the seven stars of the dipper
> The hollow of my guitar is the space between heaven and earth.
> How can I show you my style?
> You have your own young life.

Without intense experience, there can be no depth to your knowledge. The rare person who pursues their life's work opens up to the process of mastery. Through a self-realized commitment, you can confidently and fearlessly restrict your studies and, in turn, approach mastery to the depths necessary. Once you realize the interconnectedness of all things, nothing narrow exists in such an approach. Contrarily, you will touch upon the core of being, where deep realization is possible, regardless of specifics.

Mastery of one's calling paves the path to realization. Mastery results in devotion, while devotion follows repetition, and the making of a minimum of a billion mistakes. No smooth road, but one littered with the bumps and bruises of self-realization. Looking life in the eye is no easy task.

Love as Part of Mastery

The master's journey is an inward one, providing courage and insight to dig deeper and deeper. The lure to explore outwardly is eased by a sense of having returned home. Repetition becomes the means toward perception, conviction, and inevitably, profound personal expression.

In the book, *Mastery*, author George Leonard further explains,

> Genius, no matter how bright, will come to naught or swiftly burn out if you don't choose the master's journey. This journey will take you along a path that is both arduous and exhilarating. It will bring you unexpected heartaches and unexpected rewards, and you will never reach a final destination. You'll probably end up learning as much about yourself as about the skill you're pursuing.

It must certainly be said that technical excellence is a relevant and necessary facet of mastery as a whole. It is, after all, masterful technique that forms the basis of your practice. Refined technique alone, however, is not enough, it misses an essential ingredient in the recipe for mastery: spirit, the life of the master.

Brilliant technique alone can yield nothing more than finely crafted work. That is not art. If the old adage is true, art is life and life art, then a masterful life must be laden with deep truth. Depths of passion. Unabashed, courageous, intense, passionate expression. Whether citing the brilliance of an artist or that of a great human being, their merits deserve esteem in the same context. A master is a master. A masterful life is lived from the depths of one's soul, fully and deeply.

Beyond the boundaries of expert technique lies the never-ending ocean of creative expression. In that tumultuous, unpredictable sea awaits gifts for those with the vigor and foresight to seize them. Helen Keller reminds us that, "Life is a daring adventure or nothing at all."

A commitment to mastery allows us to celebrate the nuances of a simple life. The most basic experience exposes its divinity. A shadow, a pause, a quarrel, a giggle, cast miracles of an everyday, awakened life. The path toward mastery yields its own unforeseen rewards, but the love of the work is for the work itself. Your efforts must be keenly focused on your intentions.

Only one true path exists for any of us at any one time in our lives. That path can only be so on the basis of love. Love is what lights our way to ultimate contentment. "Follow your bliss," advised Joseph Campbell. I can think of no better advice. If we can clear the path toward intuition and realization, the right choices will be made.

There is no shortcut on the road to enlightenment, but there is immense joy bouncing along with a light heart and an open mind. Even though the seeds of our truest destiny are planted long before birth, life challenges us to fight the demons that seem to revel in their efforts to yank us off course. The more and the earlier on that these seeds of our being are cultivated, the more likely they will be allowed to manifest into an authentic, rewarding life of passion and purpose.

Sabrina, Huntington, New York

CHAPTER 5
SEEING WITHOUT LOOKING

Many connotations of seeing and vision have nothing at all to do with the eyes, with the physical sense. A visionary, for example, sees into the future. "I see," suggests comprehension. "I saw it coming," an intuitive experience. Ocular vision can actually hinder clear, nonjudgmental perception when infected with presumption, ignorance, or ego. Consequently, we may cheat ourselves, as bias and insecurity taint the latent gifts of a given encounter.

Photography, clearly a visual medium, actually distracts me from what my eyes see at times. My visual sense can actually hinder my ability to see *into* my subjects where I might touch upon their essential nature. This realization brought about my experiments with photographing while blindfolded.

For a period of about six months, I donned a strip of black fabric and relinquished what had been the most controlling aspect of my art, my eyesight. My awareness soared and my intuition proudly took the helm. A keen inner knowledge emerged and steered my efforts, while my heart guided the click of the shutter. For the first time, I was seeing without looking as I embraced an incredibly peaceful experience, perceiving the subtlest nuances of energy, breath, and emotion.

Vision Without Eyes

Outward appearances often stymie our ability to see into the depths of one's essence—another human being, a problem, a relationship. Every experience holds in it the potential for heightened awareness, but the truth can only present itself once your subject's and your skins have been lifted and your souls invited to dance.

A poem entitled "The Spirit Within" (author unknown) offers graceful insight:

> I am the spirit within you and I know you in all your moods
> for I am you and you are me.
> I see, I feel, I know, only through you for we are one.
> You and I grow together and the seasons come and go
> until we are still in the silence of God.

Insightfulness or Wrong Vision

We are easily led astray by surface observation. Only by pausing to deeply and compassionately penetrate the outer surface might we touch upon a subject's or situation's true nature. Unfortunately, biased views often distort our experiences through fears and fantasy. Our perceptions of actual conditions are tainted, leading us to solve the wrong problems, problems that may indeed never exist.

Have you ever found yourself criticizing an individual's behavior or a culture's customs merely because of their unfamiliarity? How often are your decisions based on your own inadequacy, ignorance, arrogance, or fear? The psychologist William James used the phrase *certain blindness* to illustrate the difficulty of people to appreciate and respect the inner meaning of another's experience. Spiritual leader Bernard of Clairvaux offered this insight most poetically when he wrote, "You wish to see; Listen."

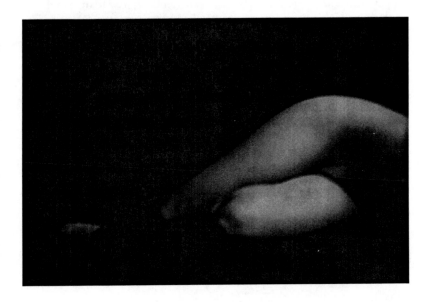

Sabrina, photographed while blindfolded

We are kept painfully separate from others if we allow our egos to contaminate our experiences. The adage, "Things are never what they appear to be," implies the need to move beyond conditioned responses, devoid of involvement or sanctimoniousness. The practice of Vipasana, clearly witnessing all things, both internally and externally, eventually leads to truth, detaching thoughts and reason from the experience. Rather, wholly *becoming* the experience.

The foundation of meditation is being in the moment: pure being, pure seeing, without recollection or assessment. A committed practice will perpetuate a heightened state of consciousness: one of consistent, conscious awareness of your present circumstance. Art making, at its best, is such a practice. It is an inner experience fluidly manifested into a tangible expression.

As an artist, I am summoned to convey the spirit of my subjects through photography. This ability allows my subjects, my viewers, and myself access to our own and each other's souls, as we all coexist on some universal plane. It offers a meditative quality of awareness derived from committed practice with a compassionate understanding and deep respect for all life. There, the cup graciously reveals its untold secrets: its sanctity.

Intention Trumps Objective Criteria

There is a delightful Zen parable about a group of five young monks who take a bicycle ride into the countryside. Upon their return, the Master asks them each of their intention. One by one, the monks are commended for their insights: finding a deeper appreciation for the wonders of nature, becoming the wind, and living in harmony with all sentient beings. Finally, the fifth monk is given his chance and replies, "I ride my bicycle to ride my bicycle." The Master sits at his feet and proclaims, "I am your student." The profundity of truly living in the moment. Experience in its pure form.

To judge anyone or anything on some objective criteria is boorish and shallow. Through practice, you may arrive at a realization that such bias cannot serve any positive end. They are based on inadequacy. Greater awareness of this judgmental tendency brings rise to compassion, where you might face the suffering of the artist through his art, the human being through his actions. You may see the depth of one's life, as well as your own, through that realization.

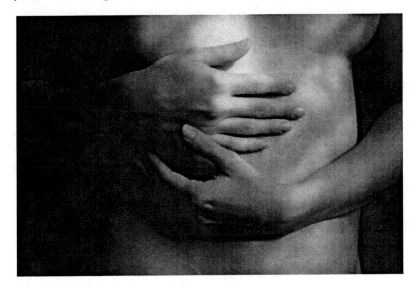

Kim, New York City

Mindfulness for Growth to See

Awareness is the first step in the transformation from self-consciousness to consciousness. From insecurity and fear, to wisdom and unhesitant, appropriate action. When fear and doubt impede the process, questioning the value and quality of our decisions, our simple, childlike responses seem unwelcome and often squelched. The ecstasy of the bike ride becomes polluted with apprehension and expectation. We lose the wondrous moment and opportunity to savor the grandest and most primitive of life's gifts, the present moment.

The reality of our frenetic world brings a trying challenge to this process, but you can surely rise above it. Intensifying the awareness of your own simple joys offers exponential reward. Savor each sacred, mystical moment. Drown in its beauty. As you do, you will open the pathway to a deeply contented, fulfilling experience. It is totally your choice. Edward Lindaman, the director of programming for the Apollo space project, offered us a gift of priceless wisdom when he wrote, "One of life's most fulfilling moments occurs in that split second when the familiar is suddenly transformed into the dazzling aura of the profoundly new." Amen.

To really see or know something, you must stand under it. From that understanding, from that perspective, judgment is out of reach. Your ego must be humbled for the truth to be seen beyond its effect on you. Do you find yourself reacting to apparent circumstances, or do you find the candor and patience to see into the heart of the matter? Do you trust yourself enough to let go and allow for a natural flow, or is your effort undue and obvious?

In photography more than anywhere else in my life, I have experienced glimpses of the harmony and balance associated with what yoga terms Samadhi, the effortless effort of awakened energy. This state of pure consciousness springs from a cultivated faith where photographs magically happen, as if I wasn't there. I realize that alas, I am not there.

Absent from the process, the egocentric *I* allows an absolute I to tap into the natural continuum of life. The art is then empowered and free to blossom. Such experiences have afforded my greatest joy as well as my most successful works. As my life coach, Marie Forleo, always reminded me, "When it's right, it's easy."

Calm and contentment flourish when we allow life to happen, accepting, cherishing, and understanding it all: the marvels and atrocities, triumph and defeat, thriving in the miracle of each moment. Remember, through mastery, by means of our initial, dedicated effort, effort may indeed ultimately cease, and fluidity and grace may abound. Thus, we are bestowed with the trust and confidence necessary to stop looking warily ahead to the future and regretfully back to the past.

In an episode of the original <u>Kung Fu</u> television series, Kwai Chang Caine, played by David Carradine, practices a series of moves. His master unexpectedly darkens the room and urges him to continue with his practice. Perplexed, Caine responds that he can't see anything, to which his master advises, "Work with what you Know, Grasshopper."

Similarly, the spirit of Star Wars' Master Obewon Kenobe counsels Luke Skywalker to stretch beyond his physical senses at his most perilous juncture, to turn inward and "Use the Force." The Force breathes an acute awareness outside of the senses that allows us to see, without looking, the awe-inspiring power of our intuition.

Our physical senses will inevitably deceive us, but with practice we can move beyond them. As children, we received lectures about the inevitable burns we would suffer from contact with fire. As adults, we perpetuate a deep-seated realization of fire's absolute danger through a belief system well rooted in life experience. But what if one of your core beliefs goes awry? How can it be that literally millions of ordinary people have walked across coal beds ranging from 1200 to 1500 degrees Fahrenheit without getting burned?

Alter Thought for Change

Moving beyond what you think you know and reflecting upon an unbiased reality offers a life beyond belief, returning to that childlike state where your reality is limited only by your imagination. Renowned Zen monk, Shunryu Suzuki, shrewdly reminds us, "In the beginner's mind there are many possibilities, but in the expert's there are few." If fire doesn't burn, then maybe cancer doesn't kill? Maybe pain is pleasure and pleasure is pain. Perhaps you are not even reading this right now.

Tolly Burkan, a foremost authority on firewalking, explains that our thoughts actually alter our brain chemistry, which in turn alters our body chemistry. Firewalkers train to pay strict attention to their thoughts, because those very thoughts create our own realities. When what we know to be true is threatened, our neurological defenses go to work and deliver a hearty dose of fear, impeding any change that might threaten our egos. We stand stilted but safe.

Recognizing fear and all of our emotions as energy enables their transformation into enlivening energy. Burkan explains, "Positive thinkers literally live in a different chemical environment than negative thinkers."

Choices Decide Who We Become

Shakespeare offered his advice, "The choices we make dictate the lives we lead." The better we feel about ourselves, the better choices we make. The right choices, those emanating from a liberated, aligned consciousness, move you in a positive direction toward success.

Erroneous choices undoubtedly bring suffering. To make intelligent choices requires that you hold faith in unforeseen potential and develop a clear and healthy mind with a degree of trust that the universe will support your cause. Spiritual practice offers the means to develop that trust and thrive in a delicate void called emptiness.

My photographs are designed to open doors for my viewers' experience and leave those doors intentionally ajar. When I have created the space necessary for you to appreciate my work through *your* experience, then I've unlocked a window to your soul. I have offered you endless ways to perceive and interpret my work. Forcing a work of art, on the one hand, demands that you see things only one way, the artist's way, my way. Your experience is manipulated and your possibilities therefore limited, emotionally, intellectually and creatively. As a result, you will receive little from the experience. Such is the stifling one-right-answer paradigm that typically characterizes education today.

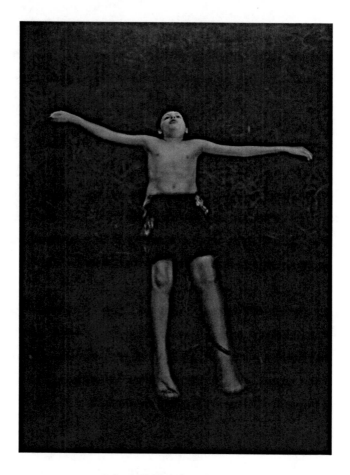

Gabriel, Hidden Acres, Connecticut

The creation of such a boundless landscape offers the artist immeasurable potential. We prefer movies with tidy endings, clear-cut solutions to problems, straight answers to questions. This concept is beautifully illustrated in Ernest Kurtz and Katherine Ketcham's book, *The Spirituality of Imperfection*: "The *perfected* is the completed, that which is finished, ended. But because we are human, we are not and *cannot* be finished or ended while we are still alive."

Such finality provides certain comfort, but leaves you timidly cornered. The real magnificence of life resides inside those questions. Inside the spaces. Between the notes. "Dwell in possibility," implored Emily Dickinson. Indeed, dwell in the moment, this fleeting moment of eternity...

Though thirty spokes may form the wheel,
it is the hole within the hub
which gives the wheel unity.
It is not the clay the potter throws
which gives the pot its usefulness
but the space within the shape
from which the pot is made
Without a door, the room cannot be entered,
and without windows it is dark.

—Tao Te Ching

Gabriel, Huntington, New York

CHAPTER 6
LIVING FROM THE HEART

My 10-year-old son Gabriel and I were walking in a crowded parking lot. He was carrying on like an absolute fool. In a wise and fatherly tone, I disappointedly remarked, "Do you realize that when you act like that, people may actually think you're mentally retarded?" I continued with my paternal counseling, "Do you care?" Gabe paused, looked me square in the eye and plainly responded, "No, as long as I'm being myself." Wise and fatherly? Try judgmental and critical! I still have so much to learn. It would have felt nice to delight in the joy of a proud teacher's work, but at that moment, all I could feel was the humility of a true beginner. I literally got down on the ground and bowed at his feet.

Who are you, really? When you touch upon your own divinity and unwrap the entangled someone you call *Me*, who are you? What remains in your nakedness after you strip away the layers of affected personality and the masks and armor? What one-of-a-kind voice flows through the heart of your heart and pulses at the core of your essential being?

A common answer to this question casts a terrorized expression, "Don't go there." Yep, it's scary stuff! Just ask your belly: "How do I feel when I realize that I've been living a life based on other people's expectations and values?"

Follow the Urge to Change

Imagine this: Your heart ignites and the passion known as living kindles down deep. You are driven by a fervent urge to burst open, to create. Hesitations cease and fears evaporate. You are truly alive in a state of pure being, engaged in wonderfully fulfilling work that prompts your absolute best. It's a beautiful image, isn't it?

It is impossible not to move in that direction when your motivation stems from your exceptionality and not from the trappings of external influence. Be forewarned, you will be awkwardly paddling against the prevailing tide of mediocrity. Your loved ones will question your ways as foreign while they painfully realize, and probably resent that you are not who you used to be. You will likely encounter distressing declarations like, "You're not the same person I married," or "You're a dreamer," or "I don't recognize you anymore." Did you think your evolution would be easy?

Just how will you cultivate the courage to embrace a deeper wisdom that compels you to push through, regardless of the discomfort? That, my friend, *is* your practice! The practice of waking up to an awareness of your divine spirit and your purpose. Waking up to the truth that the world needs your absolute best. A practice beyond the means to an end and the rhetoric of prophets and sages. You see through your fears, your defenses and the frailty of your ego, and into a heartfelt, compassionate joint venture with life, where you will finally be free, as Thoreau insisted, to "Live the life you've imagined."

A life of heightened awareness entails constant confrontation with the way things seem to be. Many take conditions for granted, while you often find yourself questioning, doubting, and searching. For what? For truth. For a level of truth that lies beneath social conformity and fear-based behavior. The pursuit requires significant courage.

Life as Art

Take a moment to consider that word, *courage*. The root word, *cor*, in Latin means heart or the seat of emotions. So, *living from the heart* actually implies having the courage to create a fully participative life with absolute honesty and integrity, regardless of circumstance. Life as a direct manifestation of your being. There is no guesswork or analysis necessary when your acts are born from the depths of your soul.

Consider your life as a work of art. Its brilliance comes alive from deep within and initially emerges through focused determination and effort. At some point though, you may find the courage to let your heart, rather than your mind and most likely your fears, direct your intentions. You surrender and welcome destiny as you realize an energy much greater than your own will. You will find yourself in a state of natural grace. Clumsy efforts cease and you step into the flow of Creation.

We typically consider courage as the strength to confront an adversary. On the rocky road of self-realization, we recognize the true adversaries as those deviously hidden within ourselves. They are the facades created by our struggle to protect our vulnerable egos and identities. These masks have deep roots and histories and may even have the ability to shape-shift. Cunning little demons.

It's the ultimate battle of Truth versus illusion. Absolute reality and presence battle the ghosts of perception. It surfaces the age-old struggle to discover your essence, embrace the real you, and allow your actions to arise from the core of your being.

Yes, living from the heart demands great courage and perseverance. It is a real challenge to stay on the path of deep knowledge and consistently strive to do what you know to be right, despite the discomfort. One way to ease that struggle is to take refuge in the kinship of like-minded practitioners. For me, that means cultivating deep friendships and a commitment to my yoga community.

When you live from your heart and your awakened consciousness guides your intentions, your mind automatically knows to create win-win conditions. From that awakened state, your benevolent actions become the ultimate gifts to both giver and receiver. Duality actually ceases, as each becomes the other. Your heart swells and you find yourself graciously sharing the absolute best of yourself— your knowledge, your wisdom, and your kindness—with no expectation of reciprocation.

Listen to Your Heart

Creative revelations are born of the heart. They are often brought about by some introspective, silent experience such as a walk, a shower, or a daydream. Significant scientific research has proven that intelligence is distributed throughout the body. In *The Other 90%*, Robert K. Cooper notes:

> When it comes to brilliance or insight, we cannot separate the body from the mind. Whenever we have a direct experience it does *not* go directly to the brain to be thought about. The first place it goes is to the neurological networks of the intestinal tract and heart.

Thus, sudden warmth in the pit of your belly, followed by a blossoming in your heart center, lets you know that an idea is on the mark.

Neurocardiologists have discovered another brain in the heart which acts independently of the head. Cooper continues, "…this heart brain is as large as many key areas of the brain in your head. It has powerful, highly sophisticated computational abilities." The heart's brain has the absolute ability to independently learn, remember, and respond to life. So it becomes quite clear that insight, mostly associated with wisdom, is first heartfelt and then brain processed.

Dedicated practice will lead you to an awareness of the subtle difference between absolute realization and intellectual rationalization. The intellect, with all its fears, doubts, and comparative logic will often sabotage your intuitive sense. Pure being, on the other hand, offers the gift of an unconditional experience and a return to our primitive sensing, untainted by reason.

In *365 Tao,* Deng Ming-Dao makes the point, "If we want simplicity and tranquility, we need only to go to the center of the spinning mind where it is empty and still." There we find ourselves with what is and where we belong. There is no need to justify these intuitive impulses. Rather, through conscientious practice, we can learn to trust in our knowing of what is right, following the path of least resistance.

If challenge number one is the intellect, then challenge number two must be the emotional body. There are, of course, those times when our emotions wreak havoc on our greater intelligence. Suddenly, and without warning, the imminent saint transforms into the demonic beast, and we are introduced to the dark side of our soul. How often have you *lost it* and lived to regret the painful words or actions unleashed?

Caught in Emotions of the Time

Emotional reactions inhibit true response through pangs of unresolved guilt, anger, sadness, or embarrassment to name a few. Although intense emotions can fuel creativity, we must nonetheless be aware of what is guiding our actions and see through the illusions masquerading as truth.

We must realize when our egos are running the show. It takes a lot more courage to admit your faults and weaknesses than it does to lash out from a wounded self-image. In a confrontation, can you find the strength to set your own stuff aside and open your heart to those who need your love and understanding? It takes strength, humility and integrity to do so, and significant effort to summon the courage to be that consciously vulnerable.

No matter what the form of expression, when I am aligned with what truly is, the work takes on a gleaming life of its own. The clumsy effort to unearth such genuineness allows for an effortless revelation of form. Glorious visions flood my mind. Photographs present themselves, calling out, "Here is the gift. I am yours for the taking."

An indefinable, incomprehensible phenomenon by any means, experience itself becomes your access to this world of wonder. Once you learn to witness your own creativity's spontaneous emergence and tap directly into the flow of creation, willful effort becomes a ridiculous notion.

Most of us, however, tend to go through life in perpetual problem-solving mode, reacting to conditions we label as negative. With a wholehearted effort to set them straight, we distort them into our preconceived notion of what is right. These challenging conditions that we are forever trying to coerce into submission become the great gurus of our lives, if we let them. Open your heart and invite them in.

To learn the lessons that these 'problems' offer, we need to step out of our stubborn egos and into the role of awakened observer. We must be willing to admit that there are myriad possibilities we've never considered. This is the basis of *vipasana* meditation or insight meditation. For a wonderful introduction to *vipasana* meditation, read *Mindfulness in Plain English* by Bhante Henepola Gunaratana. Through this practice, you will discover perspectives and choices never before considered. You will learn to see through illusion and into the heart of being.

Steps to Peace

This convoluted struggle to change the course of existence is unnecessarily painful. Who are we to say that things should be different? Instead, I would like to suggest this seven-step approach:

1. Pause. Close your eyes and take a deep, conscious inhalation...exhale.

2. Sense your body and feel into your present reality. Simply notice.

3. Keenly and quietly observe your situation as a detached witness, as if you and your condition were in separate bodies. Simply notice.

4. Accept the undeniable reality of these conditions without wishing that they were different. Simply notice.

5. Become aware of the sensations in your body. Don't make any effort to change what you feel. Simply notice.

6. Stay with your bodily sensations, releasing deeply into them, feeling them completely. Simply notice.

7. Bask in the sacred space you've just discovered, that of the present moment.

Initially, this may seem rather cumbersome, but with practice it becomes spontaneous action. The real key to the practice lies in step one, the pause. In that space, you are able to ground yourself—your mind and body—and respond with poise and candor.

In the words of Sarah Ban Breathnach from her beautiful book, *Simple Abundance: A Daybook of Comfort and Joy:*

> When the distractions of daily life deplete our energy, the first thing we eliminate is the thing we need the most: quiet, reflective time. Time to dream, time to think, time to contemplate what's working and what's not, so that we can make changes for the better...Learn how to pause.

Learning to Pause

How can we possibly recognize the prisons of deception while we're speeding along the continuum of life? There is a useful technique that I first learned from Thich Nhat Hanh where everyday occurrences act as signals to bring you back to center. Ezra Baden calls them alarm clocks and explains in his book, *At Home in the Muddy Water,* "This alarm clock is one that we ourselves set up specifically to counter the unrelenting force of our mechanical conditioning." We are jolting ourselves awake from what Baden terms "waking sleep," a habitual, delusionary state of ego-based reaction, and moving into a peaceful, meditative lull.

A traffic light, for example, can magically transform itself into a tool for mindfulness, signaling you back to your breath and body. Here is your invitation to pause, not just the spinning of your car wheels, but your mind as well. Another such alarm clock is your telephone. Instead of bounding for the phone on the first ring, allow the ring to wake you; be mindful of yourself. The phone rings and you pause...ring one...ring two...ring three...breathing in...breathing out.

Your body knows when you've slipped into an illusionary state, what spiritual teacher Eckhart Tolle fittingly terms the "pain body." What does it feel like in your body when you slip out of sacred presence and into past and future illusion? Stop for a minute and feel into it. Right now, stop and feel where in your body you hold onto conditioned beliefs and desperate hope. In your belly, your chest, your throat?

Your body cannot lie. It has no ego to protect, no personality to distort. Your body will tell you the absolute truth no matter what you *want* the truth to be. And there you have it. That detrimental source of inner conflict we more commonly call stress.

Listen to a Larger Voice

For several months, I obsessed over a particularly stagnant situation. A friend of mine had a great connection at a school where I had hoped to teach. He repeatedly offered an introduction to his colleague who could help me secure a position there. Week after week, call after call, I followed up with my friend and received nothing but excuses and aggravation, no introduction, no headway whatsoever.

Frustrated and resentful, I squandered what might have been creative energy as I assumed the role of poor little me. Yes, that is a voluntary role. I surrendered my power and was left angrily and feebly clinging to a wing and a prayer.

Then along came my friend, Patti, who patiently endured my self-pitying tale of woe. Listening intently, her eyes suddenly came aglow as she nonchalantly proclaimed, "Square peg, round hole. Walk away." Just like that, I did. Right then and there, without a speck of hindsight or regret.

Patti played the vital role of the detached witness. She was able to recognize what I could not. She understood this acquaintance as a ball and chain, preventing fluid momentum. She was also a crucial teacher in this awkward game of evolution. Balls and chains appear day in and day out, challenging us to respond from a place of wholeness and awareness. Welcome them, but see them for what they are, poignant growth opportunities.

Four days after Patti's visit, I received a call from a friend about a museum she'd stumbled upon in Baltimore, Maryland, called the American Visionary Art Museum. She sent me a link to their website and I flipped when I read their educational goals. This museum's mission exactly mirrored my own. I learned my lesson from the previous incident and this time unhesitatingly told myself I was going to Baltimore. I picked up the phone and called the museum to see who I could speak with about an idea I had for a collaborative book project.

Three days later, I was aboard Amtrak's D.C. Metroliner. That visit to Baltimore marked a defining moment in my life. In the hours spent amongst some of the most exquisite, accessible works, the vision of my greater purpose emerged with wondrous clarity. Years of seeking led me to this transformational moment. I had come home to my heart, which insisted that I seize the Baltimore opportunity.

For a peaceful change, I followed my heart. I didn't try to figure it all out. I trusted. I committed. I awoke! My soul came alive inside that museum and my purpose crystallized. I realized right then and there that the breadth of my creativity was meant to be used to awaken a spiritually sleeping society.

As a result, I took on several public art projects, a brand new arena for me. I taught photography to a group of homeless men, whose exhibition traveled continuously for three years. I created a photography exhibit for a children's art school that hung in the Long Island Children's Museum and became the content of a book entitled *Not Just Art*. I worked with a group of young boys to design and build a "peace garden" and a pair of stone benches on the grounds of their school.

With the soul ablaze, the spirit knows no bounds. The experience brought to light a profound sense of knowing that I never knew existed. Is there now a new seed of wisdom I might offer your fertile garden? Actually, it's the same as that offered by the conductor: Practice, practice, practice, so that you may remain acutely aware of the subtlest difference between life-affirming omens and deceitful temptation.

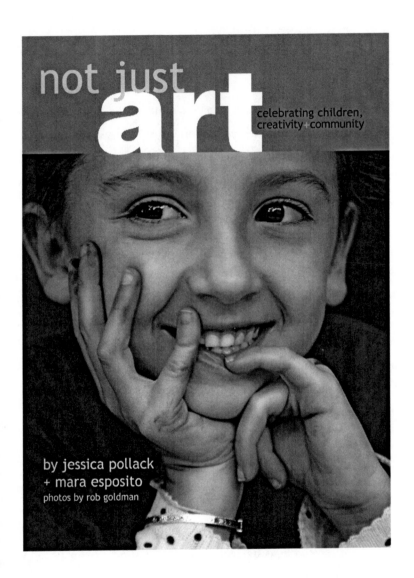

not just
art
celebrating children,
creativity, community

by jessica pollack
+ mara esposito
photos by rob goldman

CHAPTER 7
DEFINING PERSONAL SUCCESS

Will we squander away the precious minutes and hours of our day with what we have reasoned as 'important' or will we commit to the audacious pursuit of our passion? Dig deep for the truth here. I created The Energy Displacement Quotient (EDQ) as a remarkably effective tool to deal with this frustrating dilemma.

Part one of the EDQ is based on the Pauli Exclusion Principle, a physics law suggesting that no two objects can occupy the same space at the same time. In day-to-day living, there is simply not space for the coexistence of fear-driven and passion-driven action, as one displaces the other. The small stuff that loves to be sweated over miraculously dissolves as you cut off its food supply—rationalization, desperation, and doubt—and displace it with creative, aligned work. It all starts with just ten minutes a day.

Part two of the EDQ relies heavily on another physics principle, Newton's first law of motion: Unless acted upon by an unbalanced force, a body at rest will remain at rest, while a body in motion will remain in motion. Let's call this *body* your habitual routine and the *unbalanced force* your courageous resolve. As soon as you introduce the *unbalanced force* and start the ball rolling, the *body* begins its transformation from a moss-infested blob toward an energized, purposeful powerhouse. Those ten minutes a day that you initially dedicate to your most passionate work can rattle that rock free and catalyze its momentum.

Sooner than later, the miracle of part three kicks in, Motivation-Induced Time. Suddenly, you're waking up earlier with more energy. You're jotting down ideas, lyrics, and revelations on napkins and matchbooks. You coincidently meet or run into people who coincidently have just the information you need, contacts to open all the right doors. Golden opportunities start popping up from nowhere, and the next thing you know your life is changing. And maybe you're even happy. This is where creativity enters the picture as you learn to strategize your life.

My friend Ronen loves to tell people how his conference calls revolve around the high-tide schedule. An avid kayaker, he has, as he puts it, "engineered his life" to incorporate his passions into his daily agenda. This is the basis for living, not existing, and it's available to all of us whether rich, poor, young, old, married, or single. Zealous living is a state of mind. How will you find the courage, the discipline, and the perseverance to shift from a mediocre or passively acceptable existence to a vivacious one? Create it, that's how! Ten committed minutes at a time, no matter what anyone else thinks.

Steve Jobs, founder of Apple Computer and Pixar Animation Studios, offered this vital wisdom in his commencement address at Stanford University:

Your time is limited, so don't waste it living someone else's life. Don't be trapped by dogma—which is living with the results of other people's thinking. Don't let the noise of other's opinions drown out your own inner voice. And most important, have the courage to follow your heart and intuition. They somehow already know what you truly want to become. Everything else is secondary.

It begins with a decision to change the nature of your reality, affirming that from now on you will live your life with authenticity and vitality. Since I'm an undisciplined person by nature, I introduced a system into my day to support my efforts in this transformation. I discovered a marvelous book, *Aveda Rituals,* by Horst Rechelbacher, the founder of Aveda. He suggests that we consciously prepare our minds, bodies, and spirits for each day and place serious emphasis on the benefits of an intensive morning ritual. Rituals are first cousins of habits, and nurturing rituals have the potential to evolve into beneficial habits.

As I began a commitment to my morning rites, I grew to understand the power of time management as it is applied to soulful endeavors. The energy dedicated to the first hour of my day actually creates positive conditions in my mind and body, so I will respond to the challenges of my day with clarity, optimism, and a keen sense of purpose. I consider it a daily alignment with my psyche and spirit as I set the stage for success.

Discover a New Day in Ritual

My ritual evolves as I discover what works and doesn't work. It changes to suit the day's weather and by the season too. Here's an example of one of my morning rituals:

1. Waking thought: It's great to be alive! Thank you for all the wonders in my life.

2. Big Stretch and smile (inspired by my dog, Adho).

3. Read a page or two of inspirational writing from one of my favorite teachers: Thich Nhat Hanh, David Whyte, Rumi, Ralph Waldo Emerson, Eckhart Tolle, Deng Ming Dao.

4. Three-minute self massage with peppermint infused oil to wake up the body and the olfactory senses.

5. Shower with an exfoliating soap and Aveda rosemary-mint shampoo. I end my shower with about 20 seconds in ice cold water as a practice of being with what is.

6. Yoga practice and/or seated meditation for 20–90 minutes

It's like a spiritual prescription. It is delightfully addictive and it works. I encourage you to devise your own ritual so you and your family, co-workers and friends will learn the contagious nature of your positive energy. Rechelbacher's book is a solid investment. Treat yourself to a copy.

Believe in Your Dreams

Creativity works in mysterious ways. Your imaginative self can actually create something from nothing, but where do you find the courage to diligently pursue things that don't yet physically exist, your ideas and premonitions? In your heart these images are as real as anything, but to the outside world, you live in a dream. Ouch! I know that pain well.

Part of maturation is learning how to shape your heartfelt ideas in the world. First, you've got to believe in the validity of your dreams because others will not and frankly cannot. It's as if you are asking them to view a sonogram of your spirit.

If your greatest work remains locked away, the anguish is unbearable. The stagnation will bring inevitable suffering, physically, emotionally, and spiritually, while the world suffers in absence of your ultimate contributions. What does it take for you to summon the commitment and the conviction of your dreams?

When we know deep in our hearts who we really are, right action manifests fluidly from that knowing. The heart speaks and the body obeys. Decisions come from the utmost integrity and align from the get-go. We then realize peace of mind.

What happens more often than not? We are driven to seek out psycho/spiritual salvation in our neurotic, dysfunctional adulthood, to undo the damage that we have suffered as a result of misdirection and poor choices. Our bodies rebel with one stress-induced symptom after the other as we fall upon paths that perpetuate misconception and the lure of status and so-called success.

Learning How to Live

Success cannot be defined easily for the masses. Its definition is as unique as each of us. However, one universal aspect of true success makes its home within a sanctum of inner peace and authenticity. Unfortunately, as a culture, we have neglected the vital fostering of that sanctum.

In India, there is an educational and humanitarian foundation known as The Art of Living (http://www.artofliving.org). Their mission is to teach people how to revive love among themselves, improve their interpersonal relationships, and reach out to the world in a positive manner. The Art of Living works in special consultative status with the United Nations and has been embraced extensively by the education and corporate sector in India. Thanks to UNICEF, it's becoming available to the world community at large, even to the United States. India has integrated the program into mainstream society and thereby placed a priority on the education of *living*.

On the whole, we overambitious Americans have lost our sense of balance. We have a radically skewed and narcissistic notion of success that is deteriorating the very essence of our society. My wife, Carol, poignantly remarked, "I don't know anyone who's really happy." Our 'wealth' has come to be measured by the diagonal of our plasma TVs rather than our contentment, integrity, and love.

There's an illuminating line in Emerson's essay on Self-Reliance from 1841 that reads, "The civilized man has built a coach, but has lost the use of his feet." Can you imagine his take on the "civilized man" in twenty-first century Technorama? Eight, ten, and twelve step programs guaranteed to enhance your life, with systematic replacement of the simple joys of our social, creative nature.

We are unwittingly distracted from life's ultimate confrontation, the fully conscious and genuine experience of ourselves. How many people do you know who truly have a sense of belonging in the world? Seems many of us have a lot to learn about the meaning of true success. If we can summon the courage to let loose our attachment to all that we desperately grasp to in order to define ourselves, we will tap into a mystical energy that finally enables a deep thriving and a sense of what it truly means to be alive. If on the other hand, we remain obstinately fixed and fearful of a scarce and indefinite future, our energy is dispelled and our efforts paralyzed.

What I'm proposing is that we live our truth with the willingness to steep in the results of such a pursuit. A life led in this manner leaves no space for resentment. A sensitive balance of directness and compassion allows you to be cognizant of problems, misconceptions, and difficulties, while your courage grants you the ability to spontaneously deal with whatever may arise.

What would it look like to put your personality and judgment aside and engage in an absolutely egoless relationship with the world? To participate in a genuinely adult–adult conversation experiencing people and situations for what they truly are, rather than how they affect us?

That is the ultimate practice or perhaps enlightenment. Though it is our nature to steer clear of the queasiness of life, we inevitably discover that our deepest power and radiance reside in a certain courage to reveal our most fragile, vulnerable nature—the parts we warily hide in the shadows—and confront our deepest truth with unconditional candor.

This entwined dichotomy beats at the heart of my current photographs. My most haunting portraits are inarguably those in which my model has embraced the miracle of her being, absent of all effort, and summoned the strength to stand naked, literally and figuratively, with complete explanation, no labels and no excuses. Ideally, they express something rare and verbally indefinable. Like the depths of our existence.

Emma, Brooklyn, New York

Creativity or Reactivity: Your Choice for Growth

Art offers a wonderful way to shake up our tendency to grope for the known and the predictable. Works of art welcome and celebrate such ambiguity. In our lives, however, such uncertainty tends to leave us grasping for right answers. Yoga helps to pierce that predisposition, focusing our energy on the present to become intensely aware and accepting of our convoluted nature. The practice helps to curb our tendency to force our will upon the natural flow of existence.

Instead, we work to become one with all, aligning ourselves with a Universal energy where we can peacefully build upon a fertile foundation. Then and there, as naturally as cherries blossom, the seeds of a fulfilling life can be cultivated.

It is a case of creativity versus reactivity. Rather than expending time and energy to patch cracks in a marred foundation, we can choose to accept and embrace that we are who we are, however riddled with our own imperfection. Through this unconditional acceptance of our reality—right here, right now—we can breathe deeply and create space for all that is life. Obviously, this is not a practice in weaving a fairy tale existence; rather it is a gradual realization of success being a complete participation in all that is life.

The Truth Hurts...sometimes

My friend Mike is an exceptionally gifted writer. His plays have been produced on major stages, his scripts on national television. Mike is a dedicated husband and father, living a comfortable life in a cruelly expensive area. Welcome to Long Island. He makes a 'good living' as an advertising copywriter while his wife, Kathy, grins and bears her work. When did a high paying job equate with good living? He sorely protests, "We have *jobs*, not careers!"

An incubated seed of Mike's true potential was cracked open when he wrote and directed a play for his synagogue. I had the honor of sharing Mike's energy, pride, and purpose the night of that heartwarming performance where he proudly displayed remarkable talent and passion! That night, for the first time, I witnessed Mike as a truly vibrant man.

About two weeks later, he'd polished up his resume and began exploring job opportunities in positions where he could, as he said, "Make a difference in people's lives." The wheels were in motion; the rock was a rollin', and the struggle inevitably intensified as Mike's pot of potential stirred, revealing glimpses of his greater, undeniable purpose.

Time and time again, I listen deeply as people fight tooth and nail to proclaim and justify their limitations. A self-induced insistence that they choose *exclusively* between two options: a responsible, predictable, and safe path, as if there was such a thing, and a creative, passionate, unpredictable one. Sink or swim. Do or die. Why this polarized delusion?

Beneath this distorted notion lies a deep-rooted fear that our economic, social, and family positions will crumble the minute we commit to the pursuit of our dreams. I've yet to unearth any cosmic law insisting that we wait until we've secured a million dollars, educated the kids, and built a cushy retirement abode before we begin, just begin redirecting a portion of our time and energy. Even if it's just one hour a week. Ten minutes a day.

Change your intention and change your life. What you pursue will come true. These are two of my favorite mantras. You are alive and fully capable <u>right now</u>, whether you're 18 or 81! Tomorrow is as uncertain as the weather, so seize the day, or risk an undeniable and agonizing spiritual death.

Build Your Life

Take that chance because living outside of your truth hurts a lot more than a bit of ostracizing. What have you got to lose other than your pride? It only gets in your way anyhow. Consider how much you have to give when you come from a place of passion and love, and how depleted you are when you don't.

"Be the change you wish to see in the world." Gandhi's words are words to live by. That timeless wisdom is inscribed on a silver band around my wrist and reminds me to live in love every day. To live from my heart. *We* build our lives. *We* create our reality. That's the beauty of freedom. So once again, you must question your willingness to make the changes necessary to allow for a more complete life.

In the challenging voyage toward true success, there seem to be two fundamental musts: The first is wanting less; the other, commitment to do what you love as often as possible. Both require discipline and practice. It's so easy to let life slip by in the petty details. As I've become more aware of my squandered time and energy, I ache deeply to realize how much of life I sacrifice on misguided minutia. The sacred hours blindly slip by, and before we know it, it's another day, another year.

Uncomfortable questions and issues will inevitably arise as you gain insight into the absolute madness of our modern world. No doubt, the people closest to you will be threatened and confused as you are no longer the 'you' they've come to know. As the Buddha wrote, "All that is dear to me and everyone I love are of the nature to change." Change by its very nature challenges. The sooner we embrace that fact, the sooner we will surrender our unhealthy attachments to skewed perspectives, and the sooner we will take the risks necessary to bloom into our grandest capability. The choice is yours. As poet Derrick Walcott insists, "Feast on your life." Please do, the world deserves your very best.

Tessi, Huntington, NY

CHAPTER 8
BEYOND THE SUBJECT

Creativity and reactivity are clearly opposites. Creativity implies innovation and individuality, while reactivity catapults us into biased contradiction, tainted by expectations, emotions, and our predictable personalities. Creativity, on the one hand, offers us an opportunity to develop and shape our realities through a distinctively fresh experience of the world, but reactivity finds us mechanically labeling and judging, prejudiced by egoism, fear, and desire.

Creativity does not stem from what we know. It doesn't assume that we know at all. Rather, it is a bold reinterpretation of a moment-to-moment encounter with life. A spirited, real-time improvisation. Conversely, reactivity exists within a psychically agonizing battle of me versus the Universe, awkwardly twisting negative circumstances to manipulate them into safe and narrow-minded slices of life.

Blind Assumptions or Proven Strategy

What if our entire relationship to the world has been unconsciously tainted by blind assumptions of reality? Have you flown on autopilot for so long that you have lost sight of your uniquely divine purpose, your vision, and your voice? Eckhart Tolle's explanation is particularly poignant: "There's a little mind-made entity that consists entirely of thinking and accumulated thought patterns that thrives on resistance to what is."

Our torturous tendency toward deficiency-induced thoughts and actions are the basis of previous or projected results. Consequently, we miss out on innumerable opportunities for exultation right now. I recall all of those occasions where my sons have ruffled my version of how they're "supposed" to act in a given situation. Each time I catch myself robotically snapping at them, I learn and re-learn, and learn once more just how easily I succumb to old ways.

Do You Sabotage Yourself?

In Disney's The Emperor's New Groove, a peasant is tossed into the moat for carelessly interrupting the dancing emperor and throwing him *off his groove*. The wickedly, self-centered emperor, bestowed with indisputable authority, reacts the only way he knows how to the bump on his smooth road. He crushes the problem, more likely an unrecognized growth opportunity, in an effort to re-install the status quo.

Unfortunately, he fails to realize that the real problem lives within him, within his rigidity and his fear of losing control. What if he never finds his groove again? An uncertain future? Heaven forbid! Certainly not a welcome or praiseworthy condition in our goal-driven culture. The golden rule dictates: Know what you want, your goal, then set forth a surefire strategy to carry you from point A to point B, via the most expeditious route.

In the cutthroat world of business, quantifiable results rule the roost, so the SWOT analysis is used for auditing the overall strategic position of a business and its environment. A situation is evaluated based on four criteria: Strengths, Weaknesses, Opportunities, and Threats. The process helps predetermine that the most effective decisions are made to limit risk and ensure predictable results. "The purpose of strategy is to be really clear before you take the direction, says Rashi Glazer, co-director of the Center for Marketing and Technology at the University of California at Berkeley. "The point of a SWOT analysis is to have the best shot at a grounded plan,"

Such a system proves a valuable tool when sales, profits, and returns on investments motivate action. The problems crop up when such a methodology is used to manage ones life, where quantifiable results represent nothing more than a frail ego's need to define success by external means, such as wealth, status, or recognition.

Where matters of the heart are concerned, when success is defined by a degree of inner peace and contentment, an organic approach seems more viable, one that works in a certain accord with the natural world. A flow of life akin to the four seasons, migrating birds, and the waxing and waning moon. Why do we human beings, the most advanced species on the planet, tend to rebel against this organic order?

Our entire comprehension of possibility gets corrupted by a merciless calculation of ourselves and our relationship with the world. We get mired in the gooey surface of events and thrust about in our delusion of likes and dislikes, acceptance and rejection, and familiarity and aliena-tion. It's a painfully polarized existence for sure.

Open Yourself and Drink In *The Way*

A better and more favorable option would be to fully engage in life one miraculous moment at a time, to recognize and thrive in the beauty of each and every breath. In this mode we become awareness itself, a magically transformative medium. As we remain present, detached from predictably desired results, and open the channel to a fully authentic experience, we invite the raw essence of the universe to flow through us and emerge just a bit brighter and lighter, easing ourselves in the world and into alignment. Like waves on the water, independent yet com-pletely connected to the Source.

Here is the miracle; you haven't *done* a thing. You've opened your heart and embraced the genuine beauty of this phenomenon called presence. You've reached into the indefinable magnificence of existence, not the unattainable illusion with which mass media and Hollywood torture us.

We slip too easily into destructive patterns and squander priceless energy to manipulate and eradicate conditions that do not align with our truth in the first place. We're ensnared by stubborn ideals and tainted goals. As your practice begins to soften this attachment, a discriminating awareness allows for a less biased version of your experience. You will embrace certain distressing situations as welcome opportunities for awakening and growth, and dismiss others as misa-ligned distractions unworthy of consideration.

Master the skill of discernment. Your evolution requires acute attention. Empower yourself to share your very best with the world. Rather than preconceiving, learn to receive life with equanimity and wakefulness.

Life is not always reasonable, it's not always pleasant and it's not always fair. Bad news for diehard idealists like me. Sometimes you just have to trudge through the mud because the path calls for a completely different solution, one you haven't yet considered. It's a matter of detaching from a stubbornly narrow-minded stance. On the surface, it would seem best to resolve all your issues. Sometimes that's so, but oftentimes, it is time to move on.

How do you know what to do when? Your mind is just waiting for you to fall prey to its easy-way-out brand of entrapment. Only a keen consciousness will direct you to truth and free you of the lures of transient sensual pleasure, guilt alleviation, and ego boosts.

Then there's fear, a most impressive motivator. It wreaks havoc on our intelligence and moves us to do unthinkable things. Our comfort with the known keeps us locked inside our glass houses, afraid of engaging in a direct experience with life. For example, an abused wife sustains her torturous marriage despite the pain, because the familiarity offers a certain comfort. As dreadful as it is, at least she knows what to expect, and that alone offers some sense of relief.

It's what we *don't* know that scares us to death. Ironically, it's also what we don't know that holds the keys to a fulfilling life. The battered spouse demonstrates the modus operandi of the smothered, *reactive* mind, the mind whose decisions are based upon habit and trepidation rather than potentiality. As you curtail your reactive tendencies, the victim role will no longer resonate with you. Self-empowerment simply has no use for it.

Choices Make for More Pleasure than Pain

There is good and bad in all our lives—pleasure and pain, joy and sorrow—regardless of our wishes or our will. You can, however, decide how you will respond to those conditions. You can choose to retreat as a victim or push through like a sprouting seed, and evolve as a creator and a leader. Make no mistake, *you* make that choice. Healthy, aligned decisions will only arise through a diligent practice that awakens conscious behavior day after day. Easy? Surely not.

It takes an absolute commitment to the work. Don't confuse the concept of this work with drudgery or suffering. Neither should you err in the thinking that you are owed something as a result of your efforts. The Bhagavad-Gita, an ancient yoga text, explains,

> The one who is attached to the fruits of action, thinking he is doing everything, is just winding himself up. The one whose actions are devoid of design and desire for results, and whose actions are all burned by the fire of wisdom, the sages call a wise man.

In other words, deep satisfaction is derived from the work expended toward a goal, not the attainment of the goal itself. The creative process is significantly more rewarding than the end product, assuming you are acutely awake and exposed to receive the infinite beauty of presence regardless of circumstances. In an interview about my photography, I was quoted as saying, "I don't care about the photographs. I care about the moment, about the experience, and about the challenge."

When the most painful conditions, like death or divorce, make the present difficult to welcome, creating a constructive existence seems as daunting as walking without legs. Grief should not be confused with collapse. Your conditions are undeniably real and your feelings regarding them cannot be repressed. Confronting the depth of your experience is what it means to be truly alive, embracing the painful difficulty, the grit of your existence. Embracing life and desperately clinging to it are two very different notions.

Your Attention Please

It is vital that we commit to a practice that encourages wakefulness. In yoga, we're taught to reflect, correct and connect as we hold a particular pose. In photography, the same is true. As I return to outwardly familiar subjects, I'm led towards inner awareness and deeper connection, deeper understanding. Yoga and photography have become creative forms for me; they exercise my muscles of presence, physically and spiritually, awakening me toward considerate responsiveness.

Looking at the Past to Predict the Future

To understand our present condition, we've got to come to grips with our past. Not to dwell on it or brood in it, but to see it as a significant piece of the whole. Our past actions and experiences absolutely affect our present reality. Call it Karma. We cannot excuse our way out of negligent or self-destructive behavior by blaming past conditions, nor can we fantasize that they don't affect us. We must take responsibility for ourselves, neither rebelliously abandoning or desperately clinging to the past. We have a relationship with our personal history, whether we like it or not.

The very word *responsible* implies a response rather than a reaction to the conditions of our lives. Responsibility does not imply that you carry the weight of the world on your shoulders. Quite the contrary, the fair response will set you free. It all comes back to listening deeply and objectively. When you truly listen beyond the words, beneath the surface, and open to an interweaving of souls, your response is immediate and correct.

Suddenly you, your subject and the universe are seen as one without a need to second-guess or strategize a subtle or clever tactic. You are fully present in your being, where inspiring and often challenging words and actions arise from your heart.

It is our calling, our responsibility, to confront life head-on for our own good and that of the universe. Remember Marianne Williamson's wise counsel:

> Your playing small does not serve the world. There is noth-
> ing enlightened about shrinking so that other people won't
> feel insecure around you. We are all meant to shine, as chil-
> dren do. We were born to make manifest the glory of God
> that is within us.

Listen Deeply

As a Cub Scout den leader, I led six 8-year-old boys each week for an hour-and-a-half growth opportunity. One of the boys, Ron, a particularly eccentric young man, had become upset about the other boys' behavior toward him. So distressed, his mom wanted to switch him to another group. Shamefully, I admit that I was somewhat relieved about his potential departure. After all, it would make my life easier if I didn't have to deal with that inconvenience.

Then I woke up and realized that that inconvenience was a desperate little boy faced with an important crossroads in his childhood. I stood in a position to either empower or disempower him. I decided to put myself in his shoes, and instantly, I knew what to do.

To transform the boys' resentment and anger into compassion and creativity, I designed a game where they were asked to complete three sentences with three different animals: I'm most like a ..., People think I'm most like a ..., and I wish I were like a ... The boys approached the exercise very seriously, some rather apprehensively, and within a few minutes, we were engaged in a sincere conversation about mutual respect and responsibility for our actions.

I moved directly into our problem with Ron and asked each scout what specific action he was willing to take to improve the situation. Slowly but surely, after plenty of arguing and debate, each boy stepped up and presented a meaningful step that he promised to take. Needless to say, I was a proud scout leader at that moment.

It is common for our egos to become ensnared in life's challenges, often impulsively blaming others for our discontent. It's my husband's fault. It's my wife's fault. He never has anything to say. She never shuts up. He's arrogant. She's meek. News Flash, folks! It takes two to tango.

If you believe your partner has devolved and now fails to meet your expectations, what role in their demise have you played? More importantly, how will you step outside your own story, your own self-righteousness, hypocrisy, and narcissism and take a hard look in the mirror?

When I asked my son, Eli, what he could do to help with Ron's situation, he said that he had tried to tell me that there were problems, but I wasn't listening. Ouch! Wake up call! In an instant, I was forced to confront my hypocrisy and an area that I now know needs work. Thank you, Eli! I now know that I contributed to the problem as much as anyone else.

Once awakened, we realize that life's greatest lessons lie at the heart of our daily experience. They are only revealed once we've entered into a substantial conversation with the world. It's not the grand spectacles that offer transformation but the seemingly small, yet earnestly urgent gestures of kindness and love. The secret lies in a willingness to risk your comfort and apprehension, to say the awkward words and do the difficult work.

Seeking an external remedy to a chronic problem is no different than treating a psychosomatic illness with painkillers. Pain signals imbalance, John-Michael Dumais, educator and author of *Straight From the Heart* (Oak Meadow Publications, 2001) explains:

Symptoms and illness are actually intelligent processes happening within the individual. They are stories trying to unfold, trying to carry us back to ourselves, back to our essential being.

Educate yourself to see through to the roots of your problems. With that insight at hand, look deeply into your soul and acquaint yourself with the facets of your psyche you don't know, understand or may not even like. Artistic expression is a potent means for this process and the key that I've used to unlock so many doors through my Creativity Yoga® and Shooting From the Heart® programs.

Self-portrait, Bash Bish Falls, New York

Are you ready to stand naked in the immaculate terror of your own truth? You set the stage for other's creative evolution and your own when you speak and act from the heart of your condition, devoid of blame and rationale. Open, honest communication prompts the conditions for the difficult work that lies ahead. It's a weighty responsibility. It's what I call *Influential Leadership*.

I have spent years developing the courage and clarity to articulate my feelings and will continue that practice for the rest of my life. Consequently, a conversation shows the potential to crack open a door to the heart of humanity. My frankness serves as a catalyst, granting others permission to fully experience challenging aspects of *their* lives.

My photographic subjects so willingly expose their emotional underbellies because I set the stage by example. There's incredible power in the truth. There is no other way.

Once we commit to the work necessary to integrate a sense of self-confidence, self-worth, and self-love, we spontaneously invite the risks and challenges that insist on a creative approach to living. We don't fit into boxes any longer. Rather, we have returned home, awakened and alive.

Unlock the You and Travel with Others

As we expand beyond a limited perception of ourselves, we merge with a complex power that spontaneously unlocks the prison of our constraint. Finally, we realize abundance, beyond a concept but rather as an experience. We sense presence and know it as truth.

The path is simply too difficult to traverse alone, and yet, we do just that. In a perpetual state of fear and doubt, we rely on struggle relentlessly. We have lost touch with our connection to being. The scales have tipped so far toward progress that we have forgotten who we are. Without a soulful connection, we are condemned to a lonely existence. We must, as David Whyte suggests, "create a discipline of presence." In the space we create, a new voice will emerge; an authentic voice echoing the purity of spirit; a voice that speaks the language of the saints.

However we choose to approach our personal growth, we must realize the vitality of our individual contribution to the whole. We commit to a practice that leads us, as a people, toward greater balance. You must gain the confidence to legitimize your opinions, even and especially when they go against the flow. "With the realization of one's own potential and self-confidence in one's ability, one can build a better world," asserts His Holiness the 14th Dalai Lama of Tibet.

We all share in the responsibility to step up and do the arduous work. No, it is not comfortable, but willful engagement in spiritual practice prepares you for life's cruelly uninvited challenges. Consistently keeping your jaw and eyes relaxed in the face of a quivering thigh in a yoga practice prepares us for a grounded, healthy response to life's painful blows. Practice equals preparation and offers us the fortitude to confront adversity head-on.

Sure, it's more convenient to rationalize your way out of conflict and unpleasantry. How easy it is to slide away from distress, reasoning that you don't want to hurt anyone's feelings or it's not your problem? How much more challenging is it when those closest to you are affected? Cowardice does not excuse evasion. True courage fosters a gateway to compassion. It evolves on its own accord as an artless effort of an evolved conscience. We instinctively find ourselves drawn toward altruism because it is our true nature.

Life Hands Us Gifts Wrapped in Grief

Dan Greenidge dedicated considerable time shaping a group of young boys and their families. Dan was my sons' Cub Scout Master. He lived an admirable, modest life as a loving husband and father and a concerned, committed member of society. Then one day fate cast its wrath upon his gentle soul and inflicted him with a viciously degenerative illness known as A.L.S., or Lou Gherig's Disease. Within a year and a half, Dan sat paralyzed, wheelchair-bound with no more mobility than a crippled right hand. His speech arduous and strangled, he often repeated words four or five times to be understood.

So why would I initiate a deep friendship with a man in the final stages of a terminal illness? What drove me to put myself at the edge, to confront my fears and squirm in my own vulnerability? A mystical force drew me to Dan, and my experience brought me to the real understanding of brotherly love, a merging with *all* of mankind, with the vastness of eternity.

Dan offered me a sacred gift, the chance to step up and show up. He opened the door to his forbidding life where I discovered so much about my own. I must have been ready. Perhaps, all of that practice prepared me to explore and embrace a deeper understanding of my purpose. I witnessed myself through alien eyes. This was not the Rob Goldman I knew. I was discovering facets of myself completely unfamiliar, and I was utterly stupefied.

Like the magic in Dorothy's ruby slippers, she held it from the get-go, just as I held the capacity to help a dying man with my love. Yet, I was unaware of the magnitude of what was mine to give, that is, until I burned away the barricades and allowed Dan to offer me that chance. I will never be able to thank him enough for that sacred gift.

Once we find the means to step into our divine power, we quickly come to realize the absurdity of our inhibition. Martha Graham, the so-called mother of modern dance, offered these unrivaled words of wisdom to her lifelong friend, Agnes de Mille:

> There is a vitality, a life force, a quickening that is translated through you into action; and because there is only one of you in all time, this expression is unique. And if you block it, it will never exist through any other medium, and be lost. The world will not have it.

False modesty warps and weakens creative energy with discouraging assumptions and falsely perceived limitations. The internal dialogue screams out, "What will someone think of me if I tell them how I feel or disappoint them?" How many times have you carried that mind chatter, ensnared in your own trap of apprehension?

Do you find yourself presupposing people's reactions to your words or actions and consequently put off the conversation or dance around the issue? Talk about zapping energy! How often did you later find that your fearful, paranoid expectations were erroneous? You can't do the awkward external work until you've done the awkward internal work to transform your self-destructive demons into self-empowering, peaceful warriors.

Confidence Grows the Heart

Roger Staubach, the Heisman Trophy winning quarterback of the Dallas Cowboys, insisted, "Confidence doesn't come out of nowhere. It's a result of something, hours, days, weeks and years of constant work and dedication." Confidence is something we earn through perseverance and committed effort to practice. Without it, we lack the means to share valuable ideas and energy that may beget positive change.

Each and every one of us has a responsibility to become and offer our very best. We must remain steadfast on the ever-challenging path of our own evolution that true confidence, not arrogance, will be fostered. We simply cannot underestimate the vital nature of our individual contribution to society; thus, we must esteem our own worth.

The very nature of our universe is created and recreated, moment-by-moment, cell-by-cell, thought-by-thought, act-by-act. It is our thoughts, our words, and our exploits that shape the nature of our existence, not his, not hers, not theirs, but yours and mine that will unalterably determine our fate as a civilization. So we do the work necessary to arrive at a place where spontaneous action is branded with clarity, conviction, courage, and candor.

Good Pain Uncovers Realness

I spent many years as a boy lying my way out of unpleasantries. My mother's wisdom still echoes in my ears, "One lie leads to another." On one particular occasion, a tangled web of deception brought my father into the picture. An easy-going man, I proved that every person has their limits. I had lied for months about returning an overdue library book. I assumed, like any know-it-all teenager, that I could outsmart my naïve parents and concocted an ingenious scheme to prove my innocence once and for all. Lo and behold, I was foiled, and right at the pinnacle of my criminal career.

I was sentenced to solitary confinement, my room, where I remained until my father arrived home. I'm up there thinking, "No problema, Dad's a pushover." It was my mother's wrath of which I lived in fear. Then it happened. My dad entered my room, walked straight to me and in one fell swoop, slapped me across the face. I was in shock. This just didn't make sense. My father simply didn't express himself impetuously, about anything, let alone anger.

The incident stays etched in my mind as one of the tenderest moments ever shared with my dad. It was real. He was real. His *grandmotherly kindness* (referring to a Zen master awakening his unmindful student with the blow of a wooden stick) emanated directly from his heart and I received his pure, spontaneous love. A deeply shared, authentic experience taught me two unforgettable lessons: One, love is a beautifully complex phenomenon that can only be defined through firsthand experience; and two, direct, spontaneous communication makes a lasting impression for better and for worse.

Our hearts long to speak the simple truth, but our egos often carry a rather different agenda. Fear and embarrassment often stand in the way of authenticity, offering a diluted or distorted version of the truth. Be wary of the unconscious mind that speaks with candor, as these words are likely infected with bias, harmful judgment and *my way or the highway* self-righteousness. Proving other people wrong offers a false sense of empowerment as the wounded ego strategically moves to trounce a weaker foe.

Doorways to Discovery

Viewing circumstances with conscious subjectivity, fully aware of, but not governed by your emotions, allows for the realization that you may indeed be wrong. Not only is that okay, it's a beautiful doorway to deeper learning.

For learning to occur, you've got to become a tolerant listener and endure the awkwardness of your own vulnerability. In a nutshell, you've got to be willing to look like a fool. Speaking from the heart, as challenging as it may be, prompts conditions for compassion; it is *we* who walk the path of mindful living and cultivate the fertile, construc-tive grounds of co-creation that define *Influential Leadership*. We become the change we wish to see in the world.

We seem to abide by a precept that insists we can, and therefore should, personally resolve every aspect of our lives. Spirituality and faith command little if any consideration in our state-of-the-art, do-it-yourself society. Our economy relies on a system that underscores our inadequacy through incessant messages of deficiency while selling many an empty promise.

Mass media and suburban sprawl have significantly contributed to the devolution of a united people. We are mostly lonely units whose prime objective is winning. Ideals are shaken when our goals are misguided and misaligned. As we delve into spiritual practice and realize the connective nature of all things, winning loses its appeal. As your values evolve, so will your actions, intuitively. Trusting in a power and a calling greater than a frail ego offers an eased passage as you mount your next plateau.

We are truly blinded by what we know as narrow perceptions of ourselves, and the world drastically limits our potential for self-realization. Alan Watts once said, "Nirvana is where you are, provided you don't object to it." For me, Nirvana implies absolute awakening and freedom, endlessly greeting the world with the spirit of a new-born. A mind and spirit enlightened by the marvel of every smile, forever embodying the ordinary as extraordinary. In such a state, we discover the unseen, beyond the subject, and yield to our heart's astonishing vision.

In celebration of our twentieth wedding anniversary, I tied half a dozen heart-shaped doilies to fishing line which my son and I tacked to the ceiling above our bed. Months later, one romantic, candle-lit night, I discovered the mystical spirit of the paper hearts. For the first time, I saw beyond the hearts. I stared, spellbound by the unforeseen magnificence as their shadows danced upon the wall. I was open to receive the unexpected beauty of presence, like the deepened love born of a painful argument or the clever invention of a ridiculous idea, rejoicing in the awe of creation.

You Are Who You Are

When thoughts and actions are governed by paint-by-number predictability, by labels and assumption, life's freshness and vitality are shackled and damned. We must strengthen our faith and confidence to welcome the risks of experimentation. Not the thrill-seeking of bungee jumping or skydiving, but the thorny voyage of the inner landscape. In that sacred, exhilarating space, you may glimpse the veiled glory in the seemingly banal, and step upon the path of revelation.

My minimalist style of photography evolved from an equipment-laden, concept-driven, vivid potpourri of high-fashion models and tropical locations, to a single nude woman, in the same room, beside the same window, with the same black & white film, the same lens, and the same black background, time after time after time. Boring? Impossible! Challenging? Revealing? Enthralling? Yes. Yes. Yes!

Through a committed photography practice, I am able to create conditions for a consequential connection where my subject and I transcend phenomena, and I am granted access to her sacred spirit. This environment cultivation lies at the foundation of my photography. The process has forged unusually empathetic relationships between us, and I have melted the identity I so desperately clung to as a photographer.

It is amazing how important it was for me to call myself something, to be identified by what I do rather than who I am. My work is so much more about elevating consciousness through relationship than about creating photographs. It took me a long time to wrap my arms around that truth. After all, it's awfully hard to frame and sell self-realization, regardless of its pricelessness.

Seeing With Awakened Eyes

Bold, personal expression ceases to explain but rather dares to illuminate. These works become poetic documents of truth, the artist's truth, channeling the universal soul to manifest the mystical. Collective conditions reveal light through metaphor, and experiences transcend specificity. The artist, the viewer and the art stand as one.

In a state of hyper-consciousness, all of life is beautiful, the gracious and the grim. Conversely, habit and assumption taint our vision and revelation slips right through our hands. The gifts are everywhere, but only a keen awakening will grant access to the depths of this glorious existence, beyond labels, stereotypes and conventions. Only awakened eyes will see the often-disguised glory of every moment.

The fine art of conversation offers significant insight beyond the surface of language and into significance. The mechanical "Fine" to the customary "How are you?" is typically a pre-programmed cordiality that offers little or no truth. I actually refer to meaningless images in my critiques as "hello-how-are-you-fine photographs."

We all want to be heard and when we take the time to really listen, we will hear *through* the words and perceive a sense of underlying truth. Of course, misinterpretation bears risk, so the goal is not interpretation but inquiry.

Taking things at face value puts you smack dab in the middle of reaction. How can you possibly relate intelligently to anyone or anything when you haven't taken the time to listen, to understand? Spiritual practice brings us closer to our true nature where we learn to pause and awaken to our relationship with the world. In that grounded space, we breathe an artful existence, consciously, compassionately, and with purposeful intent.

Whether you're engaged with a colleague, a student, a lover, a child, a stranger or a friend, you can learn to respond mindfully and productively. As ego and expectation become less entwined in the process, the drama loses its appeal. Even in the most difficult situations, the potential for co-creation and the beauty of truth shine through. We must learn to move beyond judgment and take the time, situation by situation, to realize that generalities and assumptions are based in ignorance and arrogance and contribute nothing positive whatsoever.

Who is the Sage?

At a New York Mets game, my son and I rode a shuttle bus from a parking lot several miles away from Shea stadium. After over an hour wait in the blazing heat, a memorable experience with a 9-year-old, we finally boarded a bus. I will never forget the driver's enchanting grin as he welcomed us onboard with the sweetness and enthusiasm that one greets a lover who's been away at war. This man approached his work with such reverence and joy that he truly awoke me to the vitality available to every one of us, in every moment…regardless of circumstances.

How could I possibly place this man in the category I'd formerly labeled *bus driver*? The subject: a bus driver. Beyond the subject: a sage. It's nothing to do with status or significance or life and death situations. It is the everyday, moment-to-moment response to life that can either awaken us to the miracles of existence or blind us in prejudicial oblivion.

The reality of every circumstance is completely dependent on one's point of view. Washing the dishes, for example, helps me to become aware of my tendency to automatically place such menial tasks in the box stamped *unpleasantries*. When I approach this work with a preconceived idea that I'm going to hate it, the outcome is inevitable. I will prove myself right. When I see beyond the tedium on those occasions, I invite the possibility for a new encounter. I step inside the experience and see myself washing the dishes. I feel my body and my breath and realize that dishwashing offers rewards no less delicious than lovemaking.

Thich Nhat Hanh shares the joy he derives from a delayed flight at the airport as an invitation to meditate. While most travelers are anxiously snapping their wrists, cursing that catatonic minute hand, Thich Nhat Hanh transcends conditions and finds the space within it to call home. While others wonder when they will get there, he *is* there. He has arrived.

The situation is undeniably what it is, but your interpretation and response are your choices. How, regardless of our conditions, do we maintain a positive, peaceful, creative response to life? You got it...practice, practice, practice. You do it by dedicating yourself to a consistent spiritual practice that builds a potent foundation of awareness and integrity. You wouldn't expect to smash a homerun against a major league pitcher without years of dedicated batting practice, would you?

Mindfulness abides by the same principle. You are committing to a practice that will develop a positive, productive, compassionate response to all that life throws your way. The more demanding the pitch, the more demanding the practice.

Pause...breathe...listen...respond. It begins here.

A FINAL WORD

I have touched upon the effortless flow of life and know of its magic. Beyond my intellect, my will, and my ingenuity, flows a current of passion and abundance built on rigorous practice. Such practice insists upon a conscientious effort of connecting with the world and not ignoring or dismissing anything placed in my path. Slowly but surely I am learning that every situation holds the potential for enlightenment.

For me, photography is a spiritual practice that prompts an introspective journey. Diligent practice encourages sincere presence. Through the act of photography, I fall in love with life. My eye is awakened to the freshness and the miracle of every sight, and my vision is born anew. My subjects are no longer defined, but rather endlessly experienced. Learning photography is actually quite easy, it's learning to *see* that's difficult.

You are a creative being. Learn what it means to feel into your experience, into your being, and you will be that much closer to experiencing your truth. We must create the means to put ourselves in full contact with the substance of our existence, gulping, not sipping life, and certainly not directed by the rhetoric of any pat system. Not even mine.

Going out on a limb inevitably means falling from time to time. You will undoubtedly look foolish, alienated, unconventional, and awkward, but you won't die. Rather, you will be born. That is how we grow, by stepping into uncharted territory and inching toward the edge—the edge of what we know, what we understand, and perpetually questioning what we've been told is right and wrong, good and bad. By hazarding ourselves in a beautifully dangerous world.

Bathe in it.

Inhale it.

Savor it.

Because life, as they say, is not a dress rehearsal!

Gabriel, Lake George, New York

RESOURCES

365 Tao by Deng Ming-Dao

At Home in the Muddy Water by Ezra Bayda

Aveda Rituals by Horst Rechelbacher

Awaken the Giant Within by Anthony Robbins

Clear Mind Wild Heart by David Whyte

Hearts of Darkness directed by Eleanor Coppola

I Could Do Anything If I Only Knew What It Was by Barbara Sher

Light on Yoga by B.K.S. Iyengar

Mastery by George Leonard

Mindfulness in Plain English by Henepola Gunaratana

Not Just Art by Jessica Pollack

Peace Is Every Step by Thich Nhat Hanh

Self-Reliance an essay by Ralph Waldo Emerson

Simple Abundance by Sarah Ban Breathnach

Straight From the Heart by John-Michael Dumais

The Artists Way by Julia Cameron

The Courage to Teach by Parker Palmer

The Other 90% by Robert K. Cooper

The Path of Least Resistance by Robert Fritz

The Power of Now by Eckhart Tolle

The Spirituality of Imperfection by Ernest Kurtz and Katherine Ketcham

Who am I This Time by Jay Martin

Websites

http://www.artofliving.org

http://www.eckharttolle.com

http://www.plumvillage.org

http://www.bksiyngar.com

ABOUT ROB GOLDMAN

Rob Goldman is an internationally published photographer whose fine art, advertising, and portraiture work has been celebrated in gallery exhibitions and national magazines such as Cosmopolitan, Time, Brides, and Mademoiselle. Examples of Goldman's work can be found in both private and corporate collections including the prestigious Polaroid Collection in Waltham, Massachusetts.

Mr. Goldman has developed a variety of personal development programs for people who are ready to express their passion and their creativity in their lives and their work. His workshops and seminars are offered internationally and designed specifically for the education, business, art, and yoga communities. Rob's teaching concentrates on the human being—the artist, as a whole—encouraging and challenging people in a variety of rich, holistic, and supportive environments.

Rob Goldman's landmark programs, Shooting From the Heart® and Creativity Yoga®, integrate energies of the body, mind, and spirit, thereby releasing and focusing creative energy on all levels. Mr. Goldman also offers creativity coaching for individuals and organizations, and keynote lectures at universities, corporations, and organizations on aspects of creativity, personal development, and progressive education.

Rob Goldman's photographs have been used by Nikon, Club Med, Seagram's, AT&T, Microsoft, and Marriott, to name a few. He is founder of the Stepping Stone Gallery for Contemporary Photography in Huntington, New York, and co-founder of Art That Matters, an artist community and gallery in Oyster Bay, New York. Mr. Goldman holds an MFA in Interdisciplinary Art from Goddard College and serves on the advisory board of Suffolk County Community College's Photographic Imaging Program where he is an adjunct professor.

Mr. Goldman's most recent project is the *Just Like Me Project,* a revolutionary drug awareness program for teens. The *Just Like Me Project* empowers kids to make healthy decisions about drug use. A peer-driven approach to drug prevention, the *Just Like Me Project* helps kids rally their community around the issue of substance abuse and in the process teaches them critical life skills. To learn more, visit http://justlikemeproject.org.

You may contact Mr. Rob Goldman for a consultation at his office.

rob@rgoldman.com
http://rgoldman.com
755 Park Avenue – Suite 190
Huntington, NY 11743
Tel: 631-424-1650

NEED MORE INSPIRATION TO CHANGE YOUR LIFE?

Rob's proven signature programs will help you bust down the barriers to personal success and change your life. Decide what kind of life you want to lead and get onboard to discover your unique gifts.

Shooting from the Heart®
Defining Your Passion and Purpose

Immerse yourself in a haven of self-expression and artistic discovery. Break out of the box and tap into your limitless creative potential. Shooting From the Heart® will transform the way you see yourself and your world. This inspiring program explores the aesthetic, emotional, and spiritual aspects of photography, utilizing a unique system of insightful exercises that unleash powerfully creative energy. In an inspiring, safe, supportive environment, you'll discover newfound freedom and confidence to boldly express your inner, authentic self through personal works of photographic art. All that's needed is a solid working knowledge of your camera—any camera—and a willingness to explore your deepest source of inspiration...yourself.

Creativity Yoga®
A Guided Encounter With Your Own Creative Genius

Creativity Yoga® offers a powerful yet fun method to those ready to connect or reconnect with their passion and purpose. Get out of your overburdened mind and into your being through this unique style of yoga therapy. It is especially suited to individuals feeling creatively blocked, overwhelmed, lost or burned out, as well as those in the midst of significant life transitions. It is a deeply inspiring program that offers a stimulating method of personal and professional development. Creativity Yoga® leads people toward a more effortless, intuitive, passionate reality. First we unblock the body, then the mind, then watch the spirit take flight! Women and men with or without previous yoga experience will enjoy remarkable growth and intensified awareness through this dynamic exploration of the creative process.

Eli, Hidden Acres, Connecticut

BOOK ORDER FORM

Online: http://www.shootingfromtheheart.com **Phone:** 631-424-1650
Email book requests: orders@rgoldman.com
Mail: Rob Goldman, Inc.
         755 Park Avenue – Suite 190
         Huntington, NY 11743 USA

Name: _____

Company: _____

Address: _____

City: _____ State: ____ Postal Code: _____

Country:_____ Tel: ☐☐☐-☐☐☐-☐☐☐☐

Email: _____

☐ Check payable to: Rob Goldman, Inc.

Credit Card: ☐ **VISA**   ☐ **MasterCard**

Credit Card #: ☐☐☐☐-☐☐☐☐-☐☐☐☐-☐☐☐☐

Name on Card: _____

Signature: _____

Expiration Date: ☐☐/☐☐   Security Code: ☐☐☐☐
              Month   Year   3 or 4 digit code from back of card

Qty	Title	Unit Price	Total Price
	Shooting From The Heart	$15.95	
		Total Book Order	
		Sales Tax NY residents only add 8.625%	
		Shipping & Handling $3.50 for first book, $2.00 each additional	
		Total Amount Due	

At the center of your being
you have the answer;
you know who you are and
you know what you want.

—Lao Tzu

CPSIA information can be obtained at www.ICGtesting.com
Printed in the USA
BVOW01s0409300913

332350BV00006B/89/P